THE GRAVE
ROBBER

STUDENT
EDITION

THE GRAVE ROBBER

HOW JESUS CAN MAKE YOUR IMPOSSIBLE POSSIBLE

MARK BATTERSON
AND PARKER BATTERSON

BakerBooks

a division of Baker Publishing Group
Grand Rapids, Michigan

© 2015 by Mark Batterson and Parker Batterson

Published by Baker Books
a division of Baker Publishing Group
P.O. Box 6287, Grand Rapids, MI 49516-6287
www.bakerbooks.com

Printed in the United States of America

Library of Congress Cataloging-in-Publication Data
Batterson, Mark.
    The grave robber : how Jesus can make your impossible possible / Mark
Batterson and Parker Batterson. — Student edition.
        pages cm
    Includes bibliographical references and index.
    ISBN 978-0-8010-1597-7 (pbk. : alk. paper)
    1. Bible. John—Criticism, interpretation, etc. 2. Miracles—Biblical teaching.
I. Batterson, Parker. II. Title.
BS2615.6.M5B38 2015
226.7′06—dc23   2014040102

The authors are represented by Fedd & Company, Inc.

15 16 17 18 19 20 21   7 6 5 4 3 2 1

Contents

DON'T MISS THE MIRACLE

No one could perform the signs you are doing if God were not with him.

John 3:2

1

Dear Water: Act More Like Wine

For nearly thirty years, the One who had pieced together the universe with His voice made furniture with His hands. There's no way He wasn't a level ten carpenter, and there's no way any crooked table legs ever came out of the Nazareth woodshop.[1] But Jesus was more than a master carpenter. He was also God incognito. His miraculous power was hidden from the rest of us for thirty-some-odd years. That changed when Jesus decided some water should act a bit more like wine.

That was the day the woodbender became a waterbender. Jesus did the old switcheroo: He turned the molecular structure of water into wine—757 bottles, no less. And it was fine wine too.

Sometimes God shows up. Sometimes God shows off.

On day three of a wedding feast in Cana, that's what Jesus did. And that was just the beginning. The Gospels give us the lowdown on thirty-four miraculous highlights, but countless more went unrecorded. John's Gospel spotlights seven miracles. In a lot of ways, this is a look into seven dimensions of Jesus' miraculous power. If you've read John, you know it's like a good movie. The miracles keep getting better and better until . . . *BOOM!* Lazarus steps out of the shadow of his tomb. Who's waiting for him out there in the light? The Grave Robber Himself.

The seven miracles are seven signs, and each sign points straight to Jesus. You may be reading this book because you need a miracle. Don't we all at some point in our lives? And I'll start by saying, God wants to do *now* what He did *then*. But this is more than a course in miracles. It's a book about the only One who can perform them. So before we go any further, remember this:

Don't seek miracles.

Seek Jesus.

Seek Jesus long enough and follow Him far enough, and you'll wind up in the middle of some miracles.

Everyone wants a miracle. The problem is, no one wants to be in a situation that's so sticky they *need* a miracle (like being dead, for instance). Of course, you can't have one without the other (fear not—I'm not talking about being dead).

The prerequisite for a miracle is a problem, and the bigger the problem, the greater the potential miracle. Easy math, here. If the wedding party in Cana had tons of wine, they wouldn't have needed any more. But, fortunately, they ran out. Where the bride and groom saw a fiasco, Jesus saw an opportunity to do His thing.

The moral of the story is that nothing has changed since Jesus turned water into wine, healed a man born blind, or called Lazarus out of his tomb four days after his funeral.

He's the God who can make your impossible possible!

2

Miraculous

On a January morning in 2007, a world-class violinist played six of Bach's most stirring concertos for the solo violin on a three-hundred-year-old Stradivarius worth $3.5 million. Two nights before, Joshua Bell had performed a sold-out concert where patrons gladly paid $200 for nosebleed seats. This time, the performance was free.

Bell ditched his tux and coattails, donned a Washington Nationals baseball cap, and played incognito outside the L'Enfant Plaza Metro station (a couple stops away from my usual Metro stop!). Street musicians are not an uncommon sight or sound for Washingtonians. In fact, I (Parker) have played outside the Silver Spring Metro a time or two, usually playing more Ben Howard than Bach. Amazingly, my tip jar fared about as well as that of virtuoso Joshua Bell.

The experiment was *Washington Post* columnist Gene Weingarten's idea, and it was filmed by hidden camera. Of the 1,097 people who passed by, only seven stopped to listen. The forty-five-minute performance ended without applause or acknowledgment. Joshua Bell netted $32.17 in tips (including a $20 spot from the one person who recognized the Grammy Award–winning musician).[1]

On an average workday nearly a million passengers ride Washington's Metro system, and L'Enfant Plaza is one of the busiest stops. A stampede of tourists and government employees bustle through turnstiles, trying to get where they're going as quickly as possible. Here's the big question this little experiment raised: If we don't have one hot second to stop and listen to one of the greatest musicians in the world, playing some of the most complex, rich, diverse, robust, stirring, flavorful (you get the idea) music ever written, on one of the most beautiful instruments ever made, how many miracles do we miss during a normal day?

You've probably heard that *beauty is in the eye of the beholder.* It's true of everything, isn't it? But it's especially true of miracles. Miracles are happening all around us all the time, but you're not gonna see a thing if you're not looking for them.

The challenge is *inattentional blindness.* I'll simplify this as best I can: inattentional blindness is the failure to notice something in your field of vision because you're focused on something else. The Pharisees were a little too preoccupied with the Sabbath law, and because of that, they missed some big fat miracles happening right in front of them. Jesus healed a cripple who hadn't walked in thirty-eight years; He gave sight to a guy who was *born* blind and restored another guy's busted arm. But a bunch of the Pharisees missed the miracle, and the Messiah, because they were blinded by their legalism. They couldn't see past their religious assumptions.

Inattentional blindness is a funny thing, because it can be *intentional.* Inattentional blindness can look like *turning a blind eye to something you don't want to see* (like the Pharisees, or like a little kid who thinks you can't see him if his eyes are covered). It can also be as unintentional as *taking for granted the regular amazing stuff in your life over time.* Either way, it's one of the greatest threats to spiritual growth. On the flip side, one of the best habits you can form is learning to see the miraculous in the otherwise unexciting details of your daily life.

Mundane Miracles

Thomas Carlyle, a nineteenth-century Scottish essayist, talked about how seeing miracles in the mundane is like living your entire life in a cave and then stepping outside to witness the sunrise for the first time. He also bet that the caveman would watch the sunrise with enthralled astonishment (unlike us, who let the sun rise every day without giving a rip). In the words of G. K. Chesterton:

> Grown-up people are not strong enough to exult in monotony. Is it possible God says every morning, "Do it again" to the sun; and every evening, "Do it again" to the moon? The repetition in nature may not be a mere recurrence; it may be a theatrical encore.[2]

A few years ago, an exchange student from India rolled into National Community Church one Sunday. When meteorologists issued a winter storm warning for the DC area, he set his alarm for *three o'clock* in the morning so he wouldn't miss his first snowfall. Then he went outside, all by himself, and made snow angels in the fresh snow. He almost got frostbite because he didn't wear a jacket, a hat, or gloves. He told me he had no idea snow was that cold and that wet. I kind of laughed when he told me. But the more I thought about it, the more I thought, "Wow, I just completely ignored something he *thoroughly* enjoyed and celebrated."

When was the last time I made snow angels in the fresh snow? Or watched the sunrise as an act of worship? Or stared into the starry night sky? There are some huge fireballs up there. I rarely notice.

There is nothing like experiencing something for the first time. Firsts are important; whether it's your first snow or first kiss, the first imprint is unforgettable. There is a miraculous quality to new experiences that makes time stand still—a sneak peek of what eternity will be like.

God wired our brains to be hypersensitive to new stuff, but over time the amazing becomes routine and it's no fun anymore. We lose our awareness of the miraculous, and with it, the awe of God.

A Stellar 360

It might *seem* like you're sitting still right now (hopefully you're not reading and walking), but it's an illusion of miraculous proportions. The pale blue dot you're sitting on is spinning around its axis at a speed of roughly 1,000 miles per hour. Every 24 hours, planet Earth pulls off a *literal* stellar 360. We're also hurtling through space at an average velocity of 67,108 miles per hour. That's a heck of a lot faster than a bullet. Better yet, it's 87 times faster than the speed of sound. Feeling like you didn't get much done today? Well, you did travel 1,599,793 miles through space. Best of all, the Milky Way is spinning like a galactic pinwheel at the dizzying rate of 483,000 mph.[3]

If that isn't miraculous, I don't know what is.

Then again, when was the last time I thanked the God of the heavens for keeping us in orbit? Not recently! "Lord, I wasn't sure we'd make the full rotation today, but You did it again! Whew . . . Crisis averted." We just don't pray that way. That is some delicious irony: we already believe God for the big miracles like they're no big deal. The trick is trusting Him for the little ones like healing an incurable illness, opening a dead bolt door of opportunity, or getting us out of someone else's mess.

Compared to keeping this approximately 6,000,000,000,000,000,000,000,000-kilogram floating drop of water called Earth in orbit, how big is your biggest dream? How bad is your worst problem? How difficult is your greatest challenge?

Microscopic Miracles

You don't always need a telescope to see miracles; a microscope works just as well if you have one. Trillions of chemical reactions are taking place in your body every second of every day—you're inhaling oxygen, metabolizing energy, managing equilibrium, manufacturing hormones, fighting antigens, filtering stimuli, mending tissue, purifying toxins, digesting food, and circulating blood, to name a few. All the while your brain is performing up to ten quadrillion calculations per second using only ten watts of power.[4] That would make it the most efficient computer ever. A computer would require a gigawatt of power produced by a nuclear power plant to pull off the same performance for just a few minutes (then stuff starts melting, and that's a whole other issue).

For some reason, I know people, and so do you, who say they have never experienced a miracle. Nothing could be further from the truth. You have never *not*! You aren't just surrounded by miracles—you *are* one.

Keep looking under that microscope; things are about to get even more interesting.

If your personal genome sequence was written out longhand, it would be a three-billion-word book. The King James Version of the Bible has 783,137 words, so your genetic code is more or less four thousand Bibles. And if your personal genome sequence were an audiobook and you were read at a rate of one double helix per second, it would take nearly a century to put you into words! Psalm 139:13–14 says it best:

> You knit me together in my mother's womb.
> I praise you because I am fearfully and wonderfully made.

Those are some of the most poetic and prophetic words in the Bible. They're probably some of the oldest too. Most scholars attribute Psalm 139 to David, but one rabbinic tradition says it goes all the way back to Adam.[5] If that's true, these are some of the oldest and truest words in the history of humankind.

Every moment of every day, we experience the miraculous in the microscopic and macroscopic. Miracles are happening all around us all the time. But I would argue, you're the greatest one of all! There never has been and never will be anyone like you. Of course, this doesn't say anything about you; you were just born, a human grown inside another human, then brought safely to the outside world . . . another miracle. It does, however, say a lot about your Creator.

3

The Lost Miracles

The largest library in the world is three blocks from our church.

The Library of Congress was originally in the Capitol building until the British burned it down flat during the War of 1812.[1] Its three thousand volumes fed the fire. On January 30, 1815, Congress set out to rebuild the nation's library by approving the purchase of the largest personal collection of books in the United States, belonging to our third president, ol' Thomas Jefferson. He said it himself, "I cannot live without books."[2] Apparently he could, and he was willing to part with his 6,487 volumes for a lump sum of $23,950.

Along with its current collection of 35 million books, the Library of Congress also holds 13.6 million photographs, 6.5 million pieces of sheet music, and 5.4 million maps. Its 838 miles of bookshelves, if placed end to end, would stretch from Washington, DC, to Granite City, Illinois. Every day it's open, the library adds 11,000 new items to its collections. Housed within its vaults is one of only three perfect copies of the Gutenberg Bible (the first printed

Bible); *The Bay Psalm Book*, the first surviving book printed in the United States in 1640; "America's Birth Certificate," the 1507 world map by Martin Waldseemüller on which the name *America* appears for the first time; and the world's largest collection of historical phone books where you can find the street address and five-digit phone number of your great-great-grandparents.

One of the lesser-known books in Jefferson's collection, but maybe the most significant of all, was printed in Geneva, Switzerland, in 1555. It did quite a number on how we read the Bible. The French printer and scholar Robert Estienne had the novel idea of adding numbers to create chapters and verses. So the next time you cite Psalm 23 or Romans 8:28 or Ephesians 3:20, you have Robert Estienne's *Biblia* to thank for it. He's the guy who made "John 3:16" signs at sporting events possible. Brilliant!

This is just a guess, and I'm no historian, but I wonder if Estienne's unique translation of Scripture is what inspired Thomas Jefferson to invent his own version—*The Jefferson Bible*. Instead of adding numbers, Jefferson cut verses out. He created an abridged Bible by removing the miracles.

The Chopping Block

Thomas Jefferson was all for the teachings of Jesus, but he was also a child of the Enlightenment. When he was a sixteen-year-old freshman at the College of William and Mary, Professor William Small introduced him to the writings of the British empiricists. John Locke, Sir Francis Bacon, and their enlightened brethren were all about logic and reason. Jefferson was too.

In February 1804, Jefferson grabbed his X-Acto knife and had at it. He clipped his favorite passages out of his Bible and pasted them in double columns on forty-six octavo sheets. Jefferson included the teachings of Jesus but excluded the miracles. He nixed the virgin birth, the resurrection, and all the good stuff in between. Edwin

Gaustad said, "If a moral lesson was embedded in a miracle, the lesson survived in Jeffersonian scripture, but the miracle did not. Even when this took careful cutting with scissors."[3] The story of the man with the withered hand is a classic example. In Jefferson's Bible, Jesus still gets to have His speech about the Sabbath, but the man's hand is left unhealed. When Jefferson got to John's Gospel, Gaustad notes, he "kept his blade busy."[4] Jefferson's version of the Gospels ends with the stone rolled in front of the tomb. Jesus died on the cross but never rose from the dead. Zing!

I can't see myself going at the Good Book with scissors. That seems off, seems wrong. Then again, don't we do the same thing? We wouldn't dare use a razor, but we still cut and paste, as they say. We pick and choose our favorite verses, rolling right over the texts we don't get or don't particularly like. We rationalize the verses that are too radical. We whittle the verses that are too supernatural. We put Scripture on the chopping block of human logic and end up with a neutered gospel. And we all know that that's not "fixing" it. We commit intellectual idolatry as we try to make God in our image. And instead of living a life that resembles the supernatural standard set in Scripture, we follow an abridged version of the Bible that looks more or less like us.

The Boldest Statement in the Bible

When you knock out miracles like Thomas Jefferson did, you're left with a very wise yet very weak Jesus. That's the gimpy Jesus many people follow. He's kind and compassionate, but the raw power is MIA. So we follow His teachings but never experience His miracles. That's not just missing a part of Jesus—it's missing the point altogether.

One of the boldest statements in the Bible is in John 14:12:

> Whoever believes in me will do the works I have been doing, and they will do even greater things than these.

Greater things? I'd call that heresy if it didn't come from the lips of Jesus. It's one of those verses that we tend to rationalize, so I'm just going to go ahead and tell you what's going on here: if you follow Jesus, you'll do what He did. You'll seek to please the heavenly Father first and foremost. You'll care for the poor, wash feet, and offend some Pharisees along the way. You'll start to traffic in the miraculous. And it won't just be as an eyewitness. It'll be as the catalyst. Please believe me when I say, *you are someone else's miracle*!

Mind you: *only God can perform miracles*. So God gets all of the glory. That's a given. But as you'll see in the pages to follow, nearly every miracle has a human element. Sometimes you need to step into the Jordan River, like the priests of Israel, before God will part the waters.[5] And sometimes you need to wade into the Jordan seven times, like Naaman.[6] Only God could miraculously heal Naaman's leprosy, but Naaman would have forfeited the miracle if he hadn't positioned himself for it. His consistent obedience made it possible for God to work His magic. So while some miracles take only a single step of faith, others require multiple attempts! But whether it's ankle deep, waist deep, or neck deep, you have to get into that river. Sometimes you've gotta do the natural before God will do the supernatural.

The playground we live on, planet Earth, was designed with natural boundaries. There are outer limits of human possibility, and that's just a fact of life. The speed of light is the fence line, and the laws of nature are the fence posts. Some of them are well known, like the law of gravity or Newton's three laws of motion. Others are more obscure, like Bell's theorem. It doesn't matter, because you don't need a degree to know there are limits. It's the invisible, impassable fence between the natural and the supernatural, and no human can dig under it, climb over it, or walk around it. But, good news! God has put a gate in the fence. His name is Jesus.

If you follow Jesus long enough and far enough, you'll eventually trespass into the impossible. You'll turn water into wine, feed five thousand with two fish, and walk on water. Now, don't go walk off the nearest dock and see how many steps you can take. God will probably use His power very differently for you than He did for the original disciples. But if you believe what Jesus said, then you'll do what Jesus did. The miracles you experience can be even greater than the miracles Jesus performed, in terms of both quantity and quality. And the miracles you'll encounter in the pages that follow substantiate that statement.

Disappointment: Ain't No Thang

Maybe you've prayed for a miracle, but it feels like God didn't hear a word you said. I can't explain why some prayers aren't answered when we ask or why some miracles don't happen the way we want. But it's a mistake to allow a single disappointment to shut you down for good. Weak sauce. Disappointment is a knee-jerk reaction—we pull back on the reins of faith because we don't want to feel the sting of disappointment again.

This is subtle, but significant. So let me paint a picture.

A Swiss psychologist named Édouard Claparède was treating a forty-seven-year-old patient without short-term memory, a little over a hundred years ago. At the beginning of every appointment, they would shake hands, like normal people. Well, one day Claparède decided to perform a little experiment (all great experiments, you'll find, are little experiments). When his patient reached out her hand to shake his, he had a pin concealed in his hand, and she got pricked on the shake and quickly withdrew her hand in pain. A few minutes later, she had no memory of the pinprick. But from that moment on, she would not shake hands with Claparède. She wasn't sure why, but she felt like she couldn't completely trust him. The pain leftovers in her mind kept her from reaching her hand out.[7] Again, this is small, but really *huge*.

Think of disappointment as a pinprick. It hurts. And when we experience a disappointment in the faith department, many of us stop reaching our hand toward God. We pull back. Our trust for God just isn't there, and our dormant disappointment keeps us from reaching out in faith.

I don't think you need a brilliant psychologist to help you find out where all the doubt and disappointment come from. It's not a secret. But if you're going to experience the miraculous, you have to confront the sleeping disappointments from your past.

Remember the man who said to Jesus, "I believe; help my unbelief"?[8]

That's all of us. Am I right or am I right?

There's perpetually an internal tug-of-war between belief and unbelief. My hope is that something I write in here tugs you toward the miraculous. That's literally why John wrote his Gospel of miracles:

> But these are written that you may believe that Jesus is the Messiah, the Son of God, and that by believing you may have life in his name.[9]

The Seven Signs

The greatest miracle is the forgiveness of sin through the crucifixion and resurrection of the sinless Son of God. There isn't a close second. That miracle is available to anyone, anytime. And it's the only miracle we *must* experience if we want to spend eternity with the heavenly Father. But the miracle of salvation isn't the finish line. It's the *baseline*.

In John 2, water molecules turn into wine. Like every atom in the universe, they submit to His ultimate authority. In John 4, Jesus does a little long-distance healing showing He's the master of latitude and longitude. Then, in John 5, He reveals His mastery over chronology, reversing thirty-eight years of pain and suffering with one command. In John 6, Jesus introduces a new equation:

5 + 2 = 5,000 R12. His encore is waltzing across the waves on the Sea of Galilee. In John 9, Jesus doesn't just heal a blind man's eyes, He hard wires a blind man's brain by creating a synaptic pathway between his optic nerve and visual cortex. Boom! And just when you think you've seen it all, the Grave Robber turns a tomb into a waiting room. In John 11, four days without a pulse apparently means Lazarus still has a shot.

As Oliver Wendell Holmes once said, when a person's mind is stretched by a new idea, it never returns to its original dimensions.[10] Our exploration of the seven miracles in John's Gospel will stretch your mind, but what's more important is that you let it stretch your faith. I can tell you the facts, but I can't stretch your faith for you. That was John's original intent: to present a Gospel that can stretch our faith. The miracles of Jesus are more than *facts* of history. Every miracle is a microcosm. They don't just reveal what Jesus *did*, past tense. They reveal what He wants to *do* in your life, present tense. What He's done before, He wants to do again (and, I might add, *will* do again). And if we do what the disciples did in the Bible, God will do what He did.

Turning water into wine was epic, but it was just the beginning. Each of the seven miracles in John's Gospel is more amazing than the previous one. Each one reveals a little more power. Then the Grave Robber shows up and shows off His death-defying power. But that's just the start. The seventh miracle isn't the last chapter. Your life is. He wants to keep doing miracles through you.

Let the miracles begin.

THE FIRST SIGN

On the third day a wedding took place at Cana in Galilee. Jesus' mother was there, and Jesus and his disciples had also been invited to the wedding. When the wine was gone, Jesus' mother said to him, "They have no more wine."

"Woman, why do you involve me?" Jesus replied. "My hour has not yet come."

His mother said to the servants, "Do whatever he tells you."

Nearby stood six stone water jars, the kind used by the Jews for ceremonial washing, each holding from twenty to thirty gallons.

Jesus said to the servants, "Fill the jars with water"; so they filled them to the brim.

Then he told them, "Now draw some out and take it to the master of the banquet."

They did so, and the master of the banquet tasted the water that had been turned into wine. He did not realize where it had come from, though the servants who had drawn the water knew. Then he called the bridegroom aside and said, "Everyone brings out the choice wine first and then the cheaper wine after the guests have had too much to drink; but you have saved the best till now."

John 2:1–10

4

The Wine Maker

On the third day a wedding took place at Cana in
Galilee.

John 2:1

There are days.

Then there are days that define the rest of your life.

Some follow a predictable path, like the middle aisle of a church
on your wedding day. Others are as unpredictable as a blind date.
Either way you aren't who you were just a moment before. In a
split second, life is divided into BC and AD. The bridge to the past
is forever destroyed, and the future rushes in like a flash flood.

We all experience moments like this. Things just flip.

This was the day the tide turned for Jesus. He was cooped up
in His old man's carpentry shop for thirty-some years. For as long
as He could remember, people just called Him a carpenter. But on
the third day of a weeklong wedding feast—*bam!* Miracle time.

Flashback

The Gospels discuss thirty-four miracles. This "curriculum vitae" excludes the Big Three—the conception, resurrection, and ascension of Christ. And John himself says, straight up, at the end of the Gospels that these are just highlights and that there were actually tons more. But John chooses seven miraculous highlights, four of which are only found in *his* Gospel. Each of those seven signs reveals a new dimension of God's power, of God's personality. And they just get better and better. But before we fast-forward, let's rewind eighteen years to a defining moment when Jesus was twelve years old.

The Gospel of Luke gives us our only glimpse of the boy wonder. This is pretty much the only photo we have from Jesus' family photo album, but this one peek into His personality is like a really good trailer that previews His future.

I'll bet you have a few specific memories that stand out because they're unusual in regards to your context. Something unusual happened in a usual setting. When those opposites intersect, it's unforgettable. For Jesus, the unusual moment happened during the family's sixty-three-mile road trip from Nazareth to Jerusalem for the Passover (a big Jewish holiday).

These annual family trips probably resulted in countless childhood memories, but one moment became family folklore. Even as adults, His siblings would tease Jesus mercilessly about the day He missed the bus back to Nazareth. They would laugh about it the rest of their lives, but it wasn't funny when it happened. Mary and Joseph probably flipped out—their son went missing for *three days*! When they finally tracked Him down, Jesus was sitting in the temple courts, schooling the most brilliant minds in Israel.

And all who heard him were amazed at his understanding.[1]

He made such an impression on the small crowd that some of those same religious leaders would recognize Jesus two decades later, despite the beard and voice drop. Others would plot against His life, threatened by the spiritual capacity of the child prodigy turned miracle maker.

Since we pretty much just talk about Jesus as being the Son of God, it can be difficult to think of Jesus in human terms. But to fully appreciate His divinity, you have to realize He probably had pimples too. Jesus had to be potty-trained like every baby before Him. He had to learn everything like the rest of us. Jesus had to learn the names of the constellations He created and the laws of nature He invented. And just like us, Jesus had to discover His destiny through a relationship with His heavenly Father.

Scripture doesn't tell us how or when or where Jesus recognized that He had the power to do miracles, but I bet it wasn't at a wedding feast in Cana. Track with me here: I know it's not in the book, but I wouldn't be surprised if Jesus practiced a few miracles before they became His job. He had to have healed a few buddies while no one was watching, carved a few pieces of wood with His mind, or turned water into any number of substances before He turned it into wine. And I'm *sure* Jesus didn't make any crooked tables or chairs, because He could straighten wood simply by telling it to.

Jesus knew what He was capable of early on. So did Mary. That's why His miraculous powers rank as one of the best-kept secrets in the history of humankind. It wasn't as easy as putting on a pair of glasses like Clark Kent, but Jesus managed to act like an ordinary carpenter until the wedding at Cana. But a miracle machine can only hold it in for so long!

How hard would it have been? How could He hold in the lightning bolts when bullies took the day? How could He stand to stay on the cross when legions of angels were ready to blow the whole joint?

Yet Jesus held His hand. And that may be the greatest miracle of all: restraint. Jesus is like good poetry. His power to perform miracles is epic, but the willpower to *not* do what He was capable of doing is a heck of a lot more impressive.

The same is true for us. Restraint can be a real miracle, whether it's resisting temptation or keeping the curses in check. And Jesus set the standard! He had to deal with some ancient thugs, yet instead of annihilating His executioners, He said, "Father, forgive them, for they know not what they do."[2]

What the what? It was love that led Jesus to the cross. It was willpower that kept Him nailed there.

Story Line

My (Mark's) friend Donald Miller is legit. His *New York Times* bestseller *Blue Like Jazz* sold over a million and a half copies. For the record, my personal favorite of his is called *A Million Miles in a Thousand Years*. As a result of that book, Don founded an organization called Storyline. Its purpose is Donald's passion: to help people tell better stories with their lives.

Don recently spoke at National Community Church and shared one of the defining moments in his own story line. He was a bit of a lump during his teenage years. The way he said it was a little more blunt: "I wasn't good at anything." But, somewhere along the way, Don was asked to write a short article for his high school youth group newsletter. That's when one offhanded compliment rewrote his story line. Someone simply said, "Don, you're a really good writer." It was the first time anyone had told Don he was good at anything!

"There is always one moment in childhood," observed English playwright Graham Greene, "when the door opens and lets the future in."[3]

For me, the door opened during a sophomore speech class in high school. I pretty much gave a salvation sermon for my final project. I don't think any of my classmates got converted, but that speech became an inciting incident in my story line. Little did I know, but my mom gave a copy of that speech to my grandma, who gave a copy to her Bible study teacher. The Bible study teacher obviously liked it way more than my speech teacher. Then he asked my grandma, "Has Mark ever thought about ministry?" At that point in my plot, the answer was no. It wasn't in my version of the script. I hadn't given ministry a second thought until this compliment was relayed from my grandma to my mom to me.

Never underestimate the power of a well-timed compliment! Nothing beats it. It has the power to change a person's entire perspective on life. It has the potential to seriously change a person's plotline. Just one of those suckers can be a real miracle for someone like me or Don.

Twelve-year-old Jesus heard what was said about Him. And I'm sure He treasured those words.[4] On long afternoons in the carpenter's shop, Jesus had flashbacks to the day the door opened and let the future in. I bet He daydreamed a ton of miracles too. I know I have.

Clues

If you look back on your own history, you'll see that destiny leaves clues.

Architects started out building cities out of LEGOs. Saleswomen sold enough Thin Mints Girl Scout cookies to feed the country of Liechtenstein. Entrepreneurs cornered the lemonade stand market on their cul-de-sac. Entertainers probably lost all their Guitar Hero friends because they got so good. Teachers set up makeshift blackboards and lectured their stuffed animals. It's in us all!

Joel Buckner is a singer and songwriter at National Community Church. He's got some real skills. We invited him over for dinner one night and he shared his story with our family. Like for Jesus, the door opened for Joel when he was twelve. He sang "In Christ

Alone" by Michael English at his church and made his mama cry. I'm pretty sure his heavenly Father shed a little tear too! Nothing makes God happier than when we use our God-given gifts as tools to glorify Him.

I can only imagine the grin on God's face when Jesus turned water into wine, like when you watch your little bro hit his first homer or your baby sister ace her first recital. I can just see God slapping the nearest angel on the back and saying, "That's My boy!"

When you obsess over your sin instead of His forgiveness, it's easy to forget the fact that you're His pride and joy. For some reason, we think of ourselves as lower in importance than the lilies of the valley or the birds of the air, but according to God's taxonomy, we're just below the angels![5] And it doesn't take a miracle to make our heavenly Father proud. Sometimes all you have to do is say thanks. Sometimes all it takes is a little kiss on your earthly mom's cheek.

Hold that thought.

Saving Face

The door to the future cracked open when Jesus was twelve, but it was just a crack. He went off the grid for another eighteen years. Then the door reopened when the bar closed at the wedding. I don't know if the wedding planner didn't get enough wine or if the guests drank too much, but I'm sure a mini-crisis occurred when the bride and groom found out. Running out of wine might seem like a minor problem in the grand scheme of things, but in first-century Palestine, that's straight up public shame. Plus, your wedding day is the one day you want everything to be perfect! Can't you hear the muffled tones at the head table? *All I asked you to do was stock the bar! That's it. You knew how many people were on the guest list. I even gave you a wine list. How could you go cheapskate on our wedding day?*

Enter Jesus.

I love the fact that this first miracle of Jesus is not about saving a life. It's about saving face! And it reveals how much God cares about the minute details of our lives. God is great not just because nothing is *too big*. God is great because nothing is *too small*. If it's a big deal to you, it's a big deal to God.

A few years ago I (Mark) got to speak at the Church of the Highlands in Birmingham, Alabama. While I was there, I toured their Dream Center in downtown Birmingham to get some ideas for our Dream Center in DC. They're all about helping prostitutes, kind of like Jesus. Those prostitutes know where to turn when they have a problem. And I heard an amazing story about one of them.

One morning, the director of the Dream Center was walking out her front door on the way to work, and she felt like she should go back and grab a pair of woolly socks, like the warm ones from Costco. The feeling was so strange that she figured it might just be from God. So she tucked a pair of woolly socks in her purse and drove down to the Dream Center. She arrived to find a prostitute passed out on the front step. She carried the woman inside and called 911. As she was holding the prostitute in her arms, the woman slowly regained consciousness. That's when she asked her, "If I could get you anything, what would it be?" Without hesitation, the shivering woman said, "A pair of woolly socks." Those exact words. Come on, what are the odds? That's when she reached in her purse and pulled out her pair of woolly socks. The woman smiled and said, "They match my outfit."

Why don't miracles like that happen more often? Well, it's pretty obvious. We aren't tuned to the still small voice of the Holy Spirit. You can't hear it if you're not listening for it! The Holy Spirit is like the tuning fork (I love analogies), but we have to *listen* to Him and obey those little promptings. If we do, we'll find ourselves in the middle of miracles all the time!

Undercover Prophets

What do you think of when someone says *prophet*? You probably imagine an idiosyncratic, hookah-smoking oracle who predicts the future. By that definition, I've seen lots of "prophets" on the Metro. That isn't exactly the biblical definition or depiction. In New Testament terms, a prophet is someone who speaks words that strengthen, comfort, and encourage where needed (and as instructed by the Holy Spirit, obviously).

Jewish philosophers didn't actually believe that the prophetic gift was reserved for special individuals. Becoming prophetic was seen as the crowning point of mental and spiritual development—the more you grow spiritually, the more prophetic you become. It's as simple as seeing and seizing opportunities to make a difference in someone's life, to be so in tune with the Spirit that you can speak something with confidence about a matter you wouldn't be able to otherwise.

The youth leader who saw Donald Miller's writing potential was a prophet. So was the Bible study teacher who saw mine. And so are you. You're an undercover prophet, strategically positioned by God. And when you do speak out, it sets the stage for miracles to happen. All it takes is a word.

Mary used four words:

They have no wine.[6]

With that, Mary challenged Jesus to step into His destiny. The wine running dry in Cana was no accident. I think that's clear by now. It came disguised as a problem, but Mary saw it for what it really was—Jesus' date with destiny.

5

Six Stone Jars

They have no wine.

John 2:3 ESV

Water. Two parts hydrogen. One part oxygen.

It's the most basic chemical compound on earth. It's also the most vital. It covers 71 percent of the planet. It composes 65 percent of your body.[1]

Not everybody is Bear Grylls, but you could go twelve days without water under certain circumstances. Most of us wouldn't make it more than two or three days. However, the secret sauce (that's water) is delivered to most of us through all kinds of different faucets or spigots in and around our house, so we tend to miss how great water is. We have little gadgets that tell us the water temperature, or we can buy a deluxe showerhead to maximize water pressure. But then on the other side of the world, every twenty-one seconds, a child dies from a disease caused by unclean water.[2]

When was the last time you thanked God for good old-fashioned water?

For me (Mark), it was on the North Kaibab Trail about two miles from Phantom Ranch on the floor of the Grand Canyon. That sucker is a slow cooker. We had just run out of water, and it was 110 degrees Fahrenheit. In the shade. I quickly discovered that dehydration is mentally and physically debilitating. When we finally reached a water supply, every sip was liquid gold. You know what I'm talking about? Something tasteless just tasted so good! For the first time in my life, I saw water for what it really was—a miracle. And that's the ticket.

We don't appreciate the miracles God consistently does day in and day out. Forgive me for phrasing it this way, but the problem with God is that God is so good at what He does that we take it for granted! What God does best (like keep our planet in orbit), we often appreciate least. But if we learned to recognize the moment-by-moment miracles that are all around us all the time, we would live in wonderment every second of every minute of every day. This is all it takes to crack the joy code: joy is fully appreciating what you have, not just getting what you want. And it starts with the basics, like water.

Water has no caloric value, but it's vital to metabolism. Water is the universal solvent. It's fundamental to photosynthesis. It puts out fires. And what else would we swim in? Liquid hydrogen?

Water may be the most transparent miracle of all (pun intended). It's overlooked and underappreciated by most of us most of the time. But the first miracle isn't turning water into wine. It's water itself. Let's start there.

Degree of Difficulty

The seven miracles in John's Gospel show us the "range" of God's power. From our human vantage point, they seem to go from easy to difficult. Or maybe I should say, from impossible to impossibler. (FYI, *impossibler* won't fly in Words with Friends.) Turning water into wine is more than a magic trick, but it's not exactly as difficult as resuscitating a dead body that has been decomposing for four days! So the miracles seem to be getting progressively trickier and trickier. But then again, to an omnipotent God, there are no degrees of difficulty. There's not small, medium, large; easy, harder, hardest.

Anything's possible. *Nothing* is impossible.

When I need a miracle, I have a tendency to pray a little louder and a little longer. I pray in King James English like I'm Shakespeare or something. Or I pull out some of the Greek words I learned in seminary. But God will perpetually be unimpressed with our wording. When it comes down to it, He hears our heart more than our words. He responds to faith, not vocabulary.

What Mary *did not do* at the wedding in Cana may be as significant as what she *did do*. We're back to restraint. She didn't tell Jesus what to do or how to do it. She simply identified the problem and got Jesus involved. "They have no wine."[3]

The more trust you have, the fewer words you need. You smell what I'm stepping in here? Miracles don't depend on your ability to articulate the solution to God. There's no abracadabra. You don't need to know what to say. You just need to know where to turn, like Mary did. Mary turned to Jesus. We could probably take a page from Mary and do the same. Of course, you don't need to wait until you need a miracle.

One God Idea

I don't know the seating arrangement at the wedding in Cana, but Mary made a beeline for Jesus. That's what Steve Stewart did when he encountered a problem his engineer mind couldn't solve. Steve was asked by the Water4 Foundation to try to design a water pump that could work anywhere in the world for less than $50.

Steve had *zero* experience in hydrodynamics. In his own words, "I didn't know it wasn't possible." You're halfway to the miracle when you don't *know* that something's impossible.

Ten weeks later, after working eighteen-hour days seven days a week, Steve was more or less out of ideas. I think most engineers would be. Then he stumbled upon a Leonardo da Vinci sketch of a water pump in a book he had purchased ten years earlier while on vacation in Rome. That five-hundred-year-old doodle inspired an idea that led to a breakthrough in design. What makes that discovery miraculous is the fact that this particular sketch never got any love. This wasn't da Vinci's *Mona Lisa* or *Vitruvian Man*. In fact, despite extensive research, Steve has not been able to find it in any other books or journals. Nothing on Google Images either. It had been sitting on his shelf for a decade! God set the table for this miracle ten years before Steve even knew he'd need it.[4]

Da Vinci's original design called for a large bellows (whatever that is) and animal skins. Steve substituted PVC pipe, which you can get for cheap pretty much anywhere on earth, even in developing countries. Da Vinci's design didn't account for atmospheric pressure, which means it would be impossible for it to pump beyond thirty feet. Steve's design can pump up to a hundred feet. The cost per pump? $17.84. The Access 1.2 water pump, named after the then 1.2 billion people who didn't have access to clean drinking water, has been tested up to 3.2 million strokes without failure.[5]

This pump is more than a good idea. It's a God idea. Of course, some God ideas involve 1,260 hours of research and a random book. God ideas are like fine wine: they have to ferment for months or years or even decades before you pop the cork (unless you're Jesus, who makes it out of water in four seconds). But one God idea is worth more than a thousand good ideas. Good ideas are good, but God ideas change the course of history. Just look at Steve! In a sense Steve turned water into water—clean water. In this instance, that was a little more useful than wine. That one God idea turned out to help millions.

You're one God idea away from changing history.

Six Stone Jars

In 1934 Ole Kirk Christiansen was a Danish carpenter turned toy maker. The company he created was called LEGO, a word coined from two Danish words meaning "play well." Their motto? *Only the best is the best.* That's not a bad headline for the miracle at Cana. The master of ceremonies put it this way to the bridegroom:

> Everyone serves the good wine first, and when people have drunk freely, then the poor wine. But you have kept the good wine until now.[6]

I'd love to have seen the sheepish smile on the bridegroom's face. Jesus didn't just help him save face. He helped him put his best foot forward. Jesus didn't just save the day. He *made* the day. And the wine. That's what Jesus does best—make days. He always saves the best for last.

The raw material for the first miracle is the most basic building block in nature. It's a profound reminder that God doesn't need much to work with. In fact, He doesn't need anything. I suppose Jesus could have started with grapes and miraculously expedited the three-year fermentation process, and that would have qualified as a miracle. But by starting with water, Jesus demonstrated His ability to take the simplest thing on earth and turn it into something even more beautiful, something even more flavorful. And if God can do that with water, what can't He do? The God who spoke every atom into existence is the One who can mutate any molecule. That includes blood cells, brain cells, and cancer cells. Our cells are His LEGOs.

Ole Kirk Christiansen was quite the dreamer, but I doubt that even Ole could have imagined a flagship store in Times Square or

Legoland amusement parks across the country, not to mention a Hollywood blockbuster, video games, and themed LEGO sets that seem to make an appearance at every elementary-age birthday I've ever attended. LEGO's annual production of twenty billion bricks is outrageous. But it all started with the idea of a simple building block.

I (Mark) recently met one of the masterminds behind the LEGO brand at a gathering of entrepreneurs in Las Vegas. He gave every participant six LEGO bricks that turned into an unforgettable object lesson in ingenuity. He asked us to estimate the total number of unique combinations we could create with those six bricks. I guesstimated a few hundred, leaving me just a few hundred million short of the actual answer. I don't think anybody came anywhere close to the total number of possible combos: 915,103,765.[7]

Makes you want to play with LEGOs, doesn't it? In much the same way, we grossly underestimate the God who is able to do immeasurably more than all we can ask or imagine. Two hydrogen and one oxygen must have more combinations than we can know. And maybe that's why Jesus starts His miraculous ministry with H_2O—to show what He can do with next to nothing. The object lesson is far more unforgettable than six LEGO bricks. Start with six stone jars. Literally just add water. Bring them to Jesus.

The Fifth Force

Hundreds of chemical compounds float around in red wine, each with its own complex chemical formula. So to say that Jesus turned H_2O into C_2H_5OH via the fermentation formula would be an oversimplification.

The miracle at Cana involved a hundred chemical reactions, the most basic of which is glycolysis. In molecular terms:[8]

$$C_6H_{12}O_6 + 2\,ADP + 2\,P_i + 2\,NAD^+ \rightarrow 2\,CH_3COCOO^- + 2\,ATP + 2\,NADH + 2\,H_2O + 2\,H^+$$

How He did this, nobody knows or can explain, and that's what makes it a miracle. But it reveals His mastery and majesty at a molecular level. He's *the* catalyst for any and every transformation, whether it's turning water into wine or sinners into saints.

At last count (I'm not sure how often scientists do this), there were 10^{82} atoms in the observable universe. And every single one traces its origin back to the four words that spoke them into existence: "Let there be light."[9] God created them and God controls them. He can heal them, multiply them, or end them. He can restore a withered hand or wither a barren fig tree. That's no problemo. It's His call because it's His creation.

Abraham Kuyper, the Dutch theologian and former prime minister of the Netherlands, may have said it best: "There is not a square inch in the whole domain of our human existence over which Christ, who is Sovereign over all, does not cry, 'Mine!'"[10] I would simply substitute "subatomic particle" for "square inch." We could go smaller, but I don't want to lose the less scientifically inclined.

All things have been created through him and for him. He is before all things, and in him all things hold together.[11]

I'll make this quick: physicists have quantified four fundamental forces—gravitational, electromagnetic, strong nuclear, and weak nuclear. You know this from Physics 101. But quantum physics postulates the existence of a mysterious fifth force that governs the other four together. And perhaps they're onto something: God is the glue that binds subatomic particles together.

Every double helix is subject to its Intelligent Designer. The One who created the genetic code in the first place can most certainly crack it. But let's not forget that the laws of nature—physical, biological, and astronomical—are miracles in and of themselves. So when God overrides a law of nature that He *made*, it's really a miracle within a miracle. We shouldn't just thank Him for instantaneous healing that explodes what the medical world thinks. We should also thank Him for the healing properties of our immune system. And while we're at it, how about medical science as well? "All of the above" is the correct answer, brothers and sisters.

I (Mark) am a lifelong asthmatic, and albuterol has literally saved my life countless times. I pray for miraculous healing, but I'll be thanking God for every other miracle along the way! Even if God chooses not to heal me while on this earth, I'll never be short of breath in heaven. The One who reversed the curse of sin will reverse the curse of asthma, the curse of cancer, and the curse of Alzheimer's, or whatever it may be. Sooner or later, there will be no more pain, no more sickness, and no more death.

Wine into Blood

The first miracle foreshadows the last.

At the wedding in Cana, Jesus turned water into wine. At the Last Supper, Jesus raised a cup of wine and said, "This is my blood of the covenant, which is poured out for many for the forgiveness of sins."[12] On the eve of His crucifixion, Jesus turned an ordinary cup of wine into a bottomless glass of grace. And we all can get a sip of it. He transformed the fruit of the vine into the agent of forgiveness for every sin ever committed.

Without the shedding of blood, there was no remission of sins in the ancient Jewish sacrificial system.[13] But to reverse the curse once and for all required a sinless sacrifice. So "God made him who had no sin to be sin for us, so that in him we might become the righteousness of God."[14] It's the ultimate transformation. That is the greatest miracle of all.

When we take communion, we're remembering that miracle, that transformation. It's how we, like Mary, make a beeline to Jesus. We can drink the cup of blessing because He drank the cup of wrath.

THE SECOND SIGN

Once more he visited Cana in Galilee, where he had turned the water into wine. And there was a certain royal official whose son lay sick at Capernaum. When this man heard that Jesus had arrived in Galilee from Judea, he went to him and begged him to come and heal his son, who was close to death.

"Unless you people see signs and wonders," Jesus told him, "you will never believe."

The royal official said, "Sir, come down before my child dies."

"Go," Jesus replied, "your son will live."

The man took Jesus at his word and departed. While he was still on the way, his servants met him with the news that his boy was living. When he inquired as to the time when his son got better, they said to him, "Yesterday, at one in the afternoon, the fever left him."

Then the father realized that this was the exact time at which Jesus had said to him, "Your son will live." So he and his whole household believed.

This was the second sign Jesus performed after coming from Judea to Galilee.

John 4:46–54

6

God Speed

The official said to him, "Sir, come down before my
child dies." Jesus said to him, "Go; your son will
live." The man believed the word that Jesus spoke to
him.

John 4:49–50 ESV

In the crypt of the Capitol, there's a bronze plaque commemorating
the inventor of the telegraph, old Samuel Morse. When I first saw
it, it seemed a little misplaced. Shouldn't those walls be reserved for
politicos? But Morse had a special relationship with the Capitol.
Two decades before his history-changing invention, Morse was
commissioned to paint *House of Representatives*, a famous
depiction of a night session of Congress.

In 1825, Morse returned to Washington to paint a portrait of the
Marquis de Lafayette, the leading French supporter of the American
Revolution. While Morse was painting, a horse messenger delivered

a one-line letter from his father: "Your dear wife is convalescent." She'd fallen ill, and by the time Morse arrived in New Haven, Connecticut, his wife was buried. Haunted by the fact that he was unaware of his wife's failing health and lonely death for more than a week, Morse stopped painting and started working on a better way to do long-distance communication.

The painter-turned-inventor actually set up shop in the Capitol. Morse tested his telegraph prototype by sending messages between the House and Senate wings. According to the Senate doorkeeper, Isaac Bassett, most senators were a little skeptical, but Morse somehow snagged a $30,000 congressional appropriation to build a thirty-eight-mile telegraph line along the Baltimore and Ohio Railway from DC to Baltimore.

On May 24, 1844, a large crowd gathered inside the Capitol to witness Morse tap a message in the language he created, Morse code. Morse let Annie Ellsworth, daughter of the US Patent Commissioner Henry Leavitt Ellsworth, choose the message (smart move, Sam). The actual message (which is a sacred verse of Scripture) doesn't usually make the history books. Annie aptly chose Numbers 23:23 in the King James Version. Moments after the four-word message was received at a railroad depot near Baltimore, the same message was relayed back to the Capitol: "What hath God wrought?"

The Death of Distance

A hundred years ago, information traveled at the speed of ships, trains, and horses—i.e., not fast. Traveling seventy-five miles a day on horseback, Pony Express riders made the two-thousand-mile trip from Saint Joseph, Missouri, to Sacramento, California, in ten days flat. That's not bad, but I can make that plane ride in about six hours. Or just email ahead in six seconds! When George Washington died on December 14, 1799, it took a week for word to travel from Virginia to New York. A lot of Americans didn't get the news until the next year.

International news was a brick. Slower than slow. Newspapers sent reporters to the boat docks to gather news from passengers hopping off ocean liners. It might just be a myth, but King George supposedly made the following entry in his journal on July 4, 1776: "Nothing much happened today." Hopefully you know what happened on that day of that year. It's possible he didn't, given the fact that it took several weeks for the news of revolution to cross the pond. Sometimes the news lag had tragic consequences. Two thousand soldiers were killed in the Battle of New Orleans in 1815, two weeks after the relevant peace treaty had been signed in London.

Just a hundred years ago, the American transcontinental phone system had the capacity to handle only three simultaneous calls. The air is now layers upon layers of satelite transmissions and wifi and texts and thousands of phone calls, something our great-great-grandparents never could have imagined. We're witnessing the virtual death of time and distance. The world keeps getting smaller and smaller, faster and faster.

For those of you who aren't historically inclined, my apologies. But against that backdrop, consider the uniqueness of the second miracle. The idea of teleportation, or even *flying*, wasn't a thing in Jesus' time. It didn't cross people's minds. Most of the miracles Jesus performed were in-person encounters—toe-to-toe, hand-to-hand, and face-to-face. But just to make sure that we sometimes-less-than-smart humans know that touch isn't the key, He defied the four dimensions of space and time. It was a long-distance miracle in real time. A miracle by proxy. Jesus didn't just tap a message in Morse code; the royal official's son was healed with Jesus' *words*, even though he was twenty miles out of earshot.

Most of the eyewitnesses to this miracle knew the entire Torah by memory. I can't help but wonder if Numbers 23:23 crossed anyone's mind: "*What hath God wrought?*"

The Grand Subplot

In first-century Israel, royal officials and nomad Jewish rabbis ran in very different social circles. They avoided each other like the plague, would be more accurate. But desperate times call for desperate measures, especially when your son is at the point of death. The royal official in John 4, who probably reported to Herod himself, sought an audience with the One rumored to turn water into wine. He subjected himself to someone over whom he had political power. That kind of thing didn't really happen then. That one little "Sir" he uses may seem like a minor detail. But it shows that the royal guy was lowering himself, and I'm certain Jesus wouldn't have responded to a plea bargain based on political power. In my experience, God doesn't respond well to blackmail or bribery. But humility is the ticket, even if the request comes from a Roman bureaucrat who belonged to the wrong political party.

The first miracle at Cana was molecular. The second miracle is both physiological and geographical. There's no acetaminophen here, but Jesus kicks the fever—from twenty miles away! Many of Jesus' miracles happen via the laying on of hands, but this one is a long-distance miracle. The second miracle reveals more than His ability to regulate the hypothalamus, the brain's thermostat. It shows off His *macroscopic* mastery of time and space.

When you meet the *right* person in the *right* place at the *right* time and you have no explanation for how it happened, God may or may not be setting you up. And that is more than a subplot in Scripture. If you live a Spirit-led life, it'll become a subplot in your *life*. You can't set up supernatural synchronicities. That is God's job. But it's your job to see them and seize them. It's about being in tune.

Half a World Away

A number of years ago, I (Mark) was part of a missions trip to the Galápagos Islands (yeah, the Darwin place). We island-hopped for a week, sharing the Good News with islanders who'd never heard the gospel before.

Before going, one of our prayers was that God would set up divine appointments. I pray the same prayer every day, but I double down on missions trips. And God answered those prayers with nothing less than a keen synchronicity.

On our departure day, we got up early for a forty-five-minute bus trip across the island of Santa Cruz to catch an airport ferry to a neighboring island. Only one paved road connected the port city and the ferry, with virtually no civilization in between them. That's why we were surprised to see a hitchhiker by the side of the road in the middle of the island (the middle of nowhere). If I was behind the wheel, I would have waved and kept on trucking, but our bus driver pulled over and picked up a middle-aged man named Raul. It looked like he had been walking all night. He smelled like it too. Turns out he *had* been walking all night.

Raul could have taken a seat anywhere on the bus, but God sat him right next to one of the friendliest guys I know, Adam. He was also one of the few people on our team who spoke fluent Spanish. The seat next to Adam was open so that he could occasionally lie down because of excruciating pain in his back. We wouldn't know it until Adam visited his doctor back in DC, but he had a T12 compression fracture in his spine from cliff jumping the day before. Not fun. Despite his acute physical pain, Adam was right on board with Raul's emotional pain.

In the course of their conversation, Raul told Adam that he had considered suicide the day before. He actually tied cinder blocks around his ankles and planned on drowning himself in the ocean because his wife of thirty years had left him. Adam did more than listen to what Raul said; he understood how he felt. It had only been a few years since Adam's wife of fifteen years had left him. He too had been suicidal. Raul asked Adam how he handled the loss of his wife. Adam told him that he turned to Christ and Christ gave him a brand spankin' new life.

"God was never there for me," Raul told Adam several times, but he ended up discovering differently on August 12, 2006. God sent a busload of Americans as a divine intervention. God chose Adam for this assignment, and that one divine appointment may have been the whole reason we were there. Who knows, maybe it's the only reason Adam learned Spanish. And if it was, it was worth it, because Raul was worth it!

The Lord of Latitude strikes again.

On a human level, there's no way Adam and Raul should have ever met. You can't really manufacture those kinds of meetings. They lived in different countries and spoke different languages. They were separated by several plane rides, bus rides, and boat rides. And if it's me who just busted my spine, I'm not talking to *anyone*, no matter their pain. But the God who exists outside of our four space-time dimensions knows no spatial or chronological limitations. Setting up a divine appointment in a different hemisphere is supernaturally simple.

Someday God is going to pull back the space-time curtain and connect the dots between our prayers and His answers. Right now this just looks like a borderless blackboard with a bunch of dotted lines to me. Geometry isn't my best subject; I hope I get better in heaven. But some of those dotted lines will span millennia, like the synchronized prayers of Cornelius and Peter in Acts 10. If you are a Gentile follower of Jesus, the divine appointment between the apostle Peter and the Roman centurion, Cornelius, is one of the most important things that's ever happened to you, because Cornelius became the first non-Jewish convert. Other dotted lines will crisscross our man-made geopolitical borders, like the path of the Ethiopian eunuch who became the first missionary to his homeland. And some dotted lines will cross socioeconomic borders, like the one between Jesus and the royal official. Someday we'll see how others' prayers were answered in our lives and how our prayers were answered in others' lives.

You Go Nowhere by Accident

When I (Mark) first moved to Washington, DC, many, many years ago I had the privilege of sharing a meal with Senate Chaplain Dr. Richard Halverson. (Part of what made it unforgettable is that Muhammad Ali was eating at the table right next to us in the Senate dining room.) Dr. Halverson pastored Fourth Presbyterian Church in Bethesda, Maryland, for twenty-three years before serving the Senate. He did what pastors do—everything from preaching and counseling to marrying and burying. But he believed his most important function was pronouncing his carefully crafted benediction at the end of every service:

> You go nowhere by accident.
> Wherever you go, God is sending you.
> Wherever you are, God has put you there; He has a
>   purpose in your being there.
> Christ who dwells within you has something He wants to
>   do through you where you are.
> Believe this and go in His grace and love and power.[1]

Dr. Halverson reminded his congregation of that simple truth week in and week out until his death on December 1, 1995. Then he reminded them one last time. At the conclusion of his funeral service, Dr. Halverson himself gave the benediction via recording. There wasn't a dry eye in the place!

You go nowhere by accident.

You may not be right where *you* want to be, but God can use you right where you are. In fact, God may have you right where He wants you. That's so liberating. You don't have to get your ducks in a row first; that'll come with time. Just start doing His work! Whether you're taking a trip to Ecuador or a trip to Chipotle, God is setting up divine appointments along the way. The challenge, of course, is that they're harder to recognize closer to home because we get stuck on autopilot. Don't be in such a hurry to get where you're going that you miss the miracles along the way. Be willing to go out of your way for some miracle action.

The Seventh Hour

> So he asked them the hour when he began to get better,
> and they said to him, "Yesterday at the seventh hour
> the fever left him." The father knew that was the hour
> when Jesus had said to him, "Your son will live."
>
> John 4:52–53 ESV

In 1994, Tony Snesko moved from San Diego to Washington, DC. Tony was concerned that innocent children were being exposed to pornography simply because adult channels were one click away from cartoon channels, so he authored legislation that would force the cable industry to fully scramble pornography channels.

As Tony prepared to visit all 435 House offices, he circled the Capitol in prayer seven times. He let out a Jericho shout after the seventh circle. Needless to say, the guy was devoted. Then Tony started his door-to-door campaign. Many members applauded his efforts, but he was told it was too little, too late. The telecommunications bill he was trying to amend had already gone to markup.

There was no way the chairman of the committee would reopen the bill to include Tony's amendment because it would be reopened to anybody and everybody else's amendments too.

Tony walked out of the 220th congressional office depressed and defeated. He was feeling pretty much done, until he had a burning bush moment on the second floor of the Longworth House Office Building. As he sat on a cold marble windowsill that overlooked the Capitol, his inner self told him, *Stop wasting your time and go home to San Diego.* Then he heard the still small voice of the Holy Spirit. He recounts the experience:

> Never before, and never since, has God spoken to me so clearly. While I sat there looking down at the marble-tiled floor, totally dejected, these words were spoken to me as clear as a bell: "Who is doing this—you or Me?" I can't explain how I felt when I heard those words, but I straightened up and responded, "You are, Lord!" Instantly I was filled with more excitement than when I had first begun. At each of the following 215 offices, my presentations were given with renewed faith.[1]

When Tony made his last presentation at the Canon House Office Building, his amendment still seemed like a lost cause. But it's not over till God says it's over. Tony continues:

> I'm not exaggerating when I tell you this. As my leg crossed the threshold, right when I exited the 435th office, my pager went off. Chairman Dingle had just agreed to allow my amendment to be added to his telecommunications bill.[2]

You might have to knock on 435 doors, or walk twenty miles, but God gave you legs.

Tony got a little taste of God's impeccable timing, the same rush of adrenaline the royal official must have felt in the aftermath of his miracle. He didn't have a pager, but when he and his servants compared sundials, they realized that the miracle happened the split second Jesus proclaimed the official's son's healing twenty miles away.

Calorie Counter

I've made the twenty-mile drive from Capernaum to Cana. It's not a bad *drive*. But when was the last time you walked twenty miles? I live four blocks from my office on Capitol Hill, 437 steps door-to-door. That's not a lot of steps. I'm ashamed to admit that I drive it half the time. You may not be as lazy as I am, but twenty miles is still a fat hike. And Capernaum is seven hundred feet below sea level, so it was an uphill climb all the way to Cana.

Let me translate this miracle into calories.

I'm assuming the royal official didn't miss too many meals, given his social status. In fact, he may have had his own personal chef, valet, and butler. So he probably packed some pounds. And because this was a crisis situation, I'm sure it wasn't a slow saunter. He was hustling. Throw in a 5 percent incline one way, and my calorie counter comes up with 7,500 calories round-trip. For the sake of comparison, running a marathon at an average burn rate of 100 calories per mile would net 2,620 calories. I once burned more than 12,000 calories hiking Half Dome in Yosemite National Park, and it ranks as one of the most grueling days of my life.

My point? Some miracles take a little sweat. You're not working out till you're sweating. Your effort doesn't make miracles happen, but your lack of effort can keep them from happening. In the words of Dallas Willard, "Grace isn't opposed to effort, it's opposed to earning. Earning is an attitude. Effort is an action."[3] You cannot *earn* a miracle, but *effort* is part of the equation. You may have to hike twenty miles uphill, but the extra effort says, "Hey, I'm serious."

Are you willing to knock on 435 doors? Fill six stone jars? Hike twenty miles uphill?

Most of us follow Jesus to the point of inconvenience, but no further. We're more than willing to follow Jesus as long as it doesn't detour our plans. But look at the Good Samaritan: he was happy for a little inconvenience, and that's how he became someone else's miracle. Miracles don't happen on your way out the door; they happen off the beaten path, about twenty miles out of town.

If there is a lesson to be learned from the royal official, it's this: *if you want to experience a miracle, sometimes you've got to go way out of your way.* I'm not saying you have to make a pilgrimage, but don't wait for the miracle to come to you. It won't. Go get it. Our laziness keeps so many miracles from happening. You've got to go the extra mile. Make every effort to get in closer and closer to Jesus. That's what the woman with the issue of blood did. She fought through the crowds to touch the hem of His garment.[4] That's what the woman with the alabaster jar of perfume did. She crashed a party at a Pharisee's house.[5] That's what the four friends of an invalid did. They dropped their friend through a hole in the ceiling.[6]

Sometimes God just wants to see if you're serious!

Again and Again

Since writing *The Circle Maker*, I (Mark) have heard a lot of stories about miraculous answers to prayer. The common denominator among them is perseverance. These people just kept on trucking. Most of the people who got an answer kept circling their Jericho until the walls just . . . fell! They didn't just pray like it depended on God; they worked like it depended on them. They didn't just dream big; they prayed hard. Most of them didn't get an answer after attempt number one, but they kept praying.

Remember the story of Jesus healing the blind man with spit?[7]

It took two attempts. Even Jesus had to pray more than once! The first prayer resulted in a partial miracle, but Jesus wasn't satisfied with 20/80 or 20/40 vision. So he doubled back and prayed a second time for a 20/20 miracle: "Then Jesus laid hands on his eyes again."[8]

The operative word is *again*. What do you need to pray for again? And again and again and again? Some miracles happen in stages. If you get partial healing or partial relief, praise God for it. But don't settle for half a miracle! Keep praying for the whole miracle to happen. Sometimes we let fear keep us from praying for a miracle because we feel like we will have failed if God doesn't answer the way we want. That isn't failure, because the answer isn't up to us. The only way we can fail is failing to ask.

I've lost count of how many times I (Mark) have asked God to heal my asthma. It hasn't happened, but does that mean I quit asking? Nope. I'm pretty much okay with the fact that it's in His hands and it'll happen on *His* time. It's not my job to make the miracle happen. My job is to keep on asking. After all, God won't answer 100 percent of the prayers we don't pray.

On a recent trip to Israel, I visited the synagogue in Capernaum where Jesus performed multiple miracles. We actually held a healing service right there, and I felt like, "Hey, this is appropriate. I'll pray for healing again." If I was writing the script, I can't think of a more dramatic, TV-worthy way of finally answering my lifelong prayer. But nothing happened. I definitely felt a twinge of disappointment when I had to take my inhaler later that day, but I'm going to continue asking. When and where and how God decides to answer is His call. As long as God gives me breath to breathe, I'll keep asking.

350 Circles

If you know anything about me (Mark), you know I'm all about the circling thing. I'll keep this one short, but bear with me.

As a pastor and an author, I receive more prayer requests than I can keep track of, but I try my best to honor every single one.

Some of them represent more suffering than I can even imagine. Sometimes I just sit at my desk and cry. Others I can identify with, and that gets me in a different way. One of those requests came from a friend whose friend's son needed a lifesaving kidney transplant.

The transplant was scheduled to take place at Baptist Hospital in Oklahoma City on February 11, 2013. Just a month before the lifesaving transplant, doctors told family and friends that Marquise no longer qualified for the experimental procedure and his transplant was canceled. It was a bitter pill to swallow, but that devastating news actually steeled their determination.

The kidney donor, Paul Anderson, received a copy of *The Circle Maker* two days after the canceled procedure. He read through the night, finishing the book the next morning. That's when he started circling Baptist Hospital. Over the course of 160 days, Paul circled that hospital like it was Jericho itself. He logged more than 350 miles while circling the hospital 350 times! That's fifteen trips between Capernaum and Cana.

On June 17, 2013, Paul got his answer and Marquise got Paul's kidney.

Now here's the rest of the story.

More than a decade before, Marquise's father, Jim, shared his testimony at a men's retreat at Roman Nose State Park. One of the attendees, Paul Anderson, had no idea what he was doing there. His life was a train wreck. Paul was as far from God as you can get, but Jim's words struck the right chord at the right time.

Jim's words saved Paul's life. Thirteen years later, Paul's kidney would save Jim's son's life! Quite a web there.

Like the royal official who walked all the way to Cana, Paul walked around Baptist Hospital. At an average rate of 3 miles per hour, Paul burned approximately 125 calories per lap; 350 round trips later, that's a total of 43,750 calories!

In God's kingdom, what goes around comes around.

Back to Cana

If you've been to Disney World in Orlando, Florida, you know why going there ranks as one of the most memorable moments of my childhood. It's not called the Magic Kingdom for nothing! If I didn't know any better, I'd think there was pixie dust in the air—it's truly *the* most magical place on earth. And when it's over, the memories and emotions multiply. It's like it gets better after the fact. I guess Cana had the same effect. Maybe that's why Jesus kept going back.

Once more he visited Cana.[9]

The second miracle happened within a stone's throw of the first miracle. That can't be coincidental (if I've learned anything over the years, it's that nothing in the Bible is coincidental). Miracles often occur in space-time clusters. What I mean by that is that there are seasons and specific places where God seems to be most active, and Cana must've been one of them. It was hard for those in Cana not to have faith after Jesus' first move. I doubt they drank all 757 bottles Jesus had miraculously manufactured at the wedding feast. Some of those bottles probably became vintage collector's items for ancient connoisseurs. And whenever they uncorked a bottle, the aftertaste was pure faith.

There are places where it's hard not to have faith. That's why I pray on the rooftop of our church's coffeehouse, Ebenezer's. I tend to have a little more faith when I'm literally sitting *on top* of a miracle God has already done (turning a crackhouse into a coffeehouse). It helps me believe God for even bigger and better miracles because I'm standing on the shoulders of a past miracle.

Do you think David ever went back to the Valley of Elah where he dropped Goliath? Well, he lived right around there, so I'm sure he did. I bet Moses retraced his steps to the burning bush. I bet Peter rowed out on the Sea of Galilee to the spot where he walked on water (I know I would). Heck, Lazarus could've put flowers on the grave where he lay dead for four days.

When we forget the faithfulness of God, we lose faith. That's why it's important to constantly be reminded of the last miracle and the miracle before that and the miracle before that. It kind of forces you to look up for more.

You could put it this way: when you lose your way or lose your faith, you need to go back to the burning bushes in your life. Or your Cana. Whichever way you like.

THE
THIRD
SIGN

Some time later, Jesus went up to Jerusalem for one of the Jewish festivals. Now there is in Jerusalem near the Sheep Gate a pool, which in Aramaic is called Bethesda and which is surrounded by five covered colonnades. Here a great number of disabled people used to lie—the blind, the lame, the paralyzed. One who was there had been an invalid for thirty-eight years. When Jesus saw him lying there and learned that he had been in this condition for a long time, he asked him, "Do you want to get well?"

"Sir," the invalid replied, "I have no one to help me into the pool when the water is stirred. While I am trying to get in, someone else goes down ahead of me."

Then Jesus said to him, "Get up! Pick up your mat and walk." At once the man was cured; he picked up his mat and walked.

John 5:1–9

8

Very Superstitious

Sir, I have no one to put me into the pool when the water is stirred up, and while I am going another steps down before me.

John 5:7 ESV

In 1939, George Dantzig enrolled as a graduate student at the University of California, Berkeley, to study statistics. One of his professors was Jerzy Neyman from Poland. (Everyone had better names in the thirties!) At the beginning of one class session, Dr. Neyman chalked two examples of famously unsolvable problems on the blackboard. George happened to arrive late to class that day, and missed the warning that they were impossible. He thought the unsolvable problems were their homework, so he transcribed them in his notebook and went to work. It took a little longer than he anticipated, but George Dantzig ultimately solved both of them. On a Sunday morning six weeks later, an ecstatic Dr. Neyman knocked on George's front door to share the news. A bewildered

George actually apologized, thinking the assignment was overdue. Dr. Neyman informed George that he had solved two of statistics' unsolvable problems.[1]

With the outbreak of World War II, George Dantzig took a leave of absence from Berkeley to serve the Air Force as civilian head of the combat analysis branch. After finishing his doctorate in 1946, George returned to Washington, DC, where he worked as a mathematical adviser to the Defense Department. Then in 1966, George joined the faculty of Stanford University as professor of operations research and computer science. Dr. George Dantzig received more than a handful of awards during his distinguished career, including the National Medal of Science in 1975. For his groundbreaking research in linear programming, the Mathematical Programming Society established the George B. Dantzig award in 1982. The tools Dantzig developed have shaped the way airlines schedule their fleets, shipping companies deploy their trucks, oil companies run their refineries, and businesses manage their revenue projections. Dantzig's legacy is all over the place, but the genesis of his genius can be traced back to one moment as a statistics student. In his own words, "If someone had told me they were two famous unsolved problems, I probably wouldn't have even tried to solve them."[2]

Can you believe you didn't know who this guy is?

We make far too many false assumptions about what *is* and what *isn't* possible. George Dantzig solved those unsolvable problems because he didn't know it couldn't be done. Therein lies one of the secrets to experiencing the miraculous. In this instance, ignorance *is* bliss.

Jesus said it Himself: "With God all things are possible."[3] And just to make sure we don't miss the point, it's inverted in Luke 1:37: "Nothing will be impossible with God" (ESV). Whenever the Bible says the same thing two ways, it's usually twice as important. The word *impossible* just doesn't belong in our vocabulary: it's the primary reason we don't experience the miraculous. I let my logical assumptions trump my beliefs all the time, and I hate that! Before we know it, our reality is defined by human assumptions. That's when there *is no* divine revelation. But fear not: Jesus can make your impossible possible!

Experiencing the miraculous takes a little more than *I think I can, I think I can, I think I can.* You're not The Little Engine That Could. And it's not a Jedi mind trick. But I do think Henry Ford said it best: "Whether you think you can or think you can't—you're right." It's not mind over matter. It's faith over matter.

Faith doesn't ignore a doctor's diagnosis.

It does, however, seek a second opinion.

A Second Opinion

"You'll never walk again."

Those words echoed in his mind's ear for thirty-eight years.

Scripture doesn't reveal *how* it happened—whether it was a birth defect or genetic condition or freak accident. But the poor guy hadn't stood on his own two feet in nearly four decades.

That's a crazy long time by any measure, but it must have seemed even longer two thousand years ago when the average life expectancy was closer to twenty-eight. That average is skewed by infant mortality rates in the ancient world, but even if you lived past your second birthday, the average only rose to forty. My point? This guy was way past his prime, living on borrowed time (that's the only rapping that's going on in this book). I wonder if that's *why* Jesus singled him out. The man had been sitting by the pool of Bethesda longer than anyone could remember, but what a way for Jesus to prove that His power knows no limits. It's never too late, friends.

The invalid was out of referrals. His condition was incurable, and his case was unsolvable. But, you see, that's the Great Physician's specialty. In the face of every diagnosis the invalid had ever been given, Jesus gives a simple prescription:

Get up! Pick up your mat and walk.[4]

Have you ever watched a baby try to walk?

It's one of life's simplest comedies and greatest joys. It's not pretty. Watching a baby take those first few steps is like watching a drunk sailor walk the plank. I can just imagine how this scene played out for John. This is physical comedy at its finest. The invalid is falling all over himself at first. Those who witnessed it were laughing so hard they were crying. But those tears of laughter turned into tears of joy as they watched this disabled man do something he hadn't done in decades—jump for joy like a little child.

It doesn't matter how bad the diagnosis is. It's never too late to be who you might have been. If you're breathing, it means God's not finished with you yet. If you're not breathing, God still might not be finished yet. You're never past your prime. But if you want a second chance, you need to seek a second opinion. It's simple but not simple, if you know what I mean.

God's Got This

When Ethan was in kindergarten, a standard hearing test revealed that he had profound hearing loss in his right ear. A follow-up visit to the ear, nose, and throat specialist further revealed that his right eardrum had actually ruptured. Then a trip to Children's Hospital of Philadelphia resulted in an even more devastating diagnosis— cholesteatoma, a destructive and aggressive growth in the middle ear that would require surgery.

On June 10, 2011, Ethan underwent a seven-hour surgery to remove it. That's when doctors discovered that the growth had completely eroded his eardrum, the bones inside the eardrum, and the ear canal. It was dangerously close to crossing the brain lining.

Despite half a dozen surgeries in the span of two years, doctors concluded that his condition would require a more radical craniotomy. The thought of doctors doing open-skull surgery on their son drove Jason and Amy to their knees. But instead of allowing each surgery to shake their faith, they kept falling on their faces.

One day Amy was reading a daily devotional, *Jesus Calling*, when Ethan walked into her bedroom and asked her what it said on August 20 (his birthday). No joke, she read these words: "I am the God who heals. I heal broken bodies, broken minds, broken hearts, broken lives, and broken relationships. My very Presence has immense healing powers. You cannot live close to Me without experiencing some degree of healing."[5] She started crying the second she read it. She felt like that promise was for her, so she started circling it in prayer. By faith, Amy said to Ethan, "I believe God is telling us that He's going to heal you." She asked Ethan if he thought God would do it, and eight-year-old Ethan said, "A man can only hope!"

From that moment on, Amy's mantra was: *God's got this!*

Amy and Jason, along with their church family, started circling Ethan in prayer. Then on June 7, 2013, Ethan was rolled into the operating room. During the scheduled four-hour surgery, it was standard operating procedure for a nurse to provide updates to the family every forty-five minutes. And Ethan's nurse did just that during pre-op, but then the updates mysteriously stopped. By the sixth hour, Amy and Jason were getting nervous. When the nurse finally emerged from the operating room, she told them that the doctor wasn't giving her any information at that point. It wasn't until seven hours after Ethan was wheeled into surgery that a stupefied surgeon informed the family that there was no physical evidence of the disease. The CT scan prior to surgery was completely different from the CT scan they had done a few months before. The cholesteatoma was nowhere to be found, and the parts of the inner ear that had been completely eroded by the disease were completely regenerated. The doctor scratched his head and said there was no explanation for it. In Amy's words:

> To say I was in shock would be an understatement. We looked at each other in utter amazement. We prayed for this—hard—but we were still surprised when God answered those prayers. From what all the doctors tell us, this isn't even possible. Skull bone doesn't restore itself, and cholesteatoma cannot go away on its own. It's just not physically possible. But it's God-possible.[6]

Needless to say: God's got this!

One year after the surgery, Ethan went in for a follow-up CT scan and God did it again. The doctors had removed some of Ethan's skull as a precautionary measure, but those bones regenerated once again.

God's got this, again!

Keep Swinging

For every story of a miraculous healing like Ethan's, there are a dozen stories that don't turn out that way. Healing is the exception, not the rule. We'll talk more about it during the sixth miracle. But before we go any further, I must say again: God won't answer 100 percent of the prayers you don't pray. If you assume the answer is no, you don't even give God a chance to say yes.

If a baseball player refused to get into the batter's box because he doesn't get a hit every time up, he'd be cut in a heartbeat and his salary would "miraculously" disappear. But that's how many of us approach prayer. We let a few strikeouts keep us from crushing homers! Believe me, my prayer batting average is no better than anyone else's. I whiff all the time, but if I'm going down, I'm going down swinging.

Ty Cobb, one of baseball's all-time great hitters, had a life-time batting average of .367. When he was in his seventies, Cobb participated in an old-timers game and a reporter purportedly asked him, "What do you think you'd hit if you were playing major league baseball today?"

Cobb said, "About .310, maybe .315."

The reporter surmised, "That's because of travel, night games, artificial turf, and new pitches like the slider, right?"

Cobb said, "No. I'd only hit .300 because I'm seventy-two years old."[7]

I love that mindset.

Great hitters have selective memories—that goes for both baseball and life. No matter how many times you strike out, faith keeps swinging for the fences. If you want to experience the miraculous, you have to come to terms with the fact that who, what, when, where, and how aren't up to you. You can't really answer your own prayers. Sorry. But if you fail to ask God, He cannot answer them either!

It looks to me like most miracles happen to the people who make the fewest assumptions. Joshua didn't assume that the sun couldn't stand still.[8] Elisha didn't assume that iron ax heads don't float.[9] Mary didn't assume that virgins don't get pregnant.[10] Peter didn't assume water isn't walkable.[11] Best of all, Jesus didn't assume that death was the end of life.[12]

You'll make fewer and fewer assumptions the more you grow in faith.

The Wrong Miracle

When I (Mark) was in the eighth grade, some people from Calvary Church in Naperville, Illinois, came knocking on my family's front door. We were new to the church, and they wanted to know if there was anything about which we could "agree in prayer." I had a chronic case of asthma that had resulted in half a dozen hospitalizations throughout my childhood, so we asked them to pray that God would heal me.

Several decades later, I still have asthma. But something wild happened that night. When I woke up the next morning, all the warts on my feet were completely gone! I kid you not. My first thought was that there must have been some sort of confusion between here and heaven because I definitely didn't get what I ordered. And that's when I heard the inaudible yet unmistakable voice of God for the first time in my life: "I just wanted you to know that I am able."

God is able.

That's my only assumption.
And any other assumption is a false assumption.
I don't hear the voice of God as often or as clearly as I would like. And guessing the will of God can feel like a game of pin the tail on the donkey. But it is difficult to doubt after an experience like that. God doesn't always answer my prayers how I want or when I want, but I live with an unshakable conviction that God is able.

Five Fingers

The last time our family was in Ethiopia, my friend Zeb Mengistu told us about a recent flurry of healing miracles. One of the disjointing things about visiting a country like Ethiopia is the number of people with very visible physical deformities. They just don't have surgical solutions for their problems like we do in the United States.

The physical needs are very similar, in size and scope, to the ones Jesus would have encountered two thousand years ago. And maybe that's why physical healing is more common in third world countries than first world countries. Of course, it might have something to do with the fact that they have more faith and make fewer assumptions. They don't know what God can't do!

During our visit, Pastor Zeb shared about one of the documented healings. A boy with no fingers on one hand was brought to a healing service. His hand literally had five stubs, but they still prayed for him. The pastor who was leading the service prayed for the boy, then turned around and walked away. That's when he heard a pop, followed by another and another and another and another. The crowd started cheering as they saw five new fingers pop out of the boy's hand.

Why don't we witness miracles like that?

One simple answer is the false assumption that they won't happen or can't happen! We don't have the faith to even ask, so we can count these kinds of miracles on one hand. But if we had more faith, we might see a few more miracles that are biblical-level freaky.

False Assumptions

Modern archaeological excavations have uncovered what is believed to be the ancient pool of Bethesda. Located near the Sheep Gate, the two-pool complex was twenty feet deep and as large as a football field. Surrounded by five roofed colonnades that provided shade from the Middle Eastern sun, it was like the first-century Israel mall—everyone gathered here.

For thirty-eight years, a handicapped parking permit hung in our protagonist's window. He had a reserved spot at the pool of Bethesda. Day in and day out, he begged for money from bathers. It was rare that they made eye contact with him, even rarer that they gave him a handout. But one thing kept him coming back. Every once in a blue moon, the waters would be stirred. We know now that the cause of the stirring was probably the intermittent springs that fed the pool, but a superstition grew up around the stirring. Some believed that the stirring was caused by angels. And the first one into the water after the water was stirred was the winner.

Like a bad scene from a tragicomedy, hundreds of invalids would creep and crawl and claw their way to the water, hoping they'd be the first ones there. But the real tragedy was that it wasn't even true! It didn't matter whether they were first or last. It was false hope based on a false assumption. It's easy to be dismissive of silly superstitions: we all know someone who wears their lucky socks on game day, plays the lottery on their birthday, and is very cautious about making plans on Friday the 13th. We all have our pet superstitions. But a lot of times with God, these little superstitions prevent anything supernatural from actually happening. Anything less than 100 percent reliance on the miraculous power of God and God alone short-circuits the supernatural.

The opposite of belief isn't just unbelief.

It's false belief.

The invalid's greatest handicap wasn't physical. His most debilitating handicap was mental—a false assumption that he needed to be the first one into the pool of Bethesda when the water was stirred. And we make the same mistake, don't we? We keep trying what isn't working. What we need is someone to get in our face and ask us: *How's that working for you?*

If you want God to do a new thing, you can't keep doing the same old thing. If you want to experience the miraculous, you need to unlearn every assumption you've ever made, save one:

God is able. True dat.

9

Self-Fulfilling Prophecies

Do you want to get well?

John 5:6

Dr. Evan O'Neill Kane performed more than four thousand surgeries during his distinguished career as chief surgeon at Kane Summit Hospital. But his medical masterpiece was as a pioneer in the use of local anesthesia. Dr. Kane believed that general anesthesia was an unnecessary risk for patients with heart conditions and allergic reactions, so he set out to prove his point by performing major surgery using nothing more than a local anesthesia. On February 15, 1921, his patient was prepped for surgery and wheeled into the operating room. After a local anesthetic was administered, Dr. Kane cut the patient open, clamped the blood vessels, removed the patient's appendix, and stitched the wound. Two days after surgery, the patient was released from the hospital. The patient was none other than Dr. Evan O'Neill Kane. Didn't see that coming, did

73

you? His self-surgery changed standard operating room procedure forever.

Up until the 1968 Olympic Games in Mexico City, world-class high jumpers used the straddle technique, the Western roll, or the scissors jump. Then along came Dick Fosbury. After the self-surgery story, you probably know where this is going. None of those traditional techniques suited his six-foot-five-and-a-half-inch body type, so Fosbury experimented with a shoulders-first, face-up technique. His high school coach flipped (not literally), but Fosbury went on to win the gold medal in Mexico and set a new Olympic record of seven feet, four-and-a-quarter inches. At the next Olympic games, twenty-eight out of forty competitors used the technique named after the man who changed his sport forever—the Fosbury Flop.

On July 29, 1588, the Spanish Armada sailed into the English Channel with the goal of turning Great Britain into a Spanish state. Spain was the world's greatest naval power at the time, and the armada of 130 ships was called the Invincible Fleet. The English were outnumbered and outgunned, but they unveiled a new tactic of naval combat that changed the rules of engagement. For all of you who've always wondered, "When did using cannons start?" this is it. Instead of boarding enemy ships and engaging in hand-to-hand combat, the English used long-range cannons to sink half of the Spanish fleet without losing a single ship of their own.

You get the gist. If you want to repeat history, do it the way it's always been done. If you want to change history, do it the way it's never been done before. History makers are rule breakers! And no one was better at it than the One who wrote the rules in the first place.

Point-Blank

The ability of Jesus to formulate the perfect questions that we see peppered across the Gospels is nothing short of art. He could've whooped Socrates in the Socratic method. Imagine playing twenty questions with this guy. The ability to read minds, which He whips out a time or two, is an unfair advantage.

The Gospels record 183 questions, depending on your translation of choice. While they fall into a wide variety of categories, some of the most poignant are the point-blank ones. One of these point-blankers is the catalyst for the third miracle. Jesus asks an invalid:

Do you want to get well?[1]

On one level, the question seems kind of mean, doesn't it? Like adding insult to injury. Of course he wants to get well! But that isn't an assumption Jesus made. He knew better. You can't help someone who doesn't want help, no matter how badly they need it. The thief on the cross, the one throwing around insults, is a case in point. He was somewhere between six and twenty feet from salvation, but he cursed the only one who could have helped him.[2]

Over the years, I've gotten to know quite a few people who live on the streets of Washington, DC. We've shared meals, sometimes stories. And one of the painful truths I've come to realize is that some people want help, but others don't. And it's not just people living on the streets. You can't help those who won't even help themselves, no matter who they are. Some of my homeless friends have gotten homes and gotten jobs. In fact, one of them helps lead our homeless ministry at National Community Church. But for every success story, there are still some who resist change, even change for the better.

It's easy to become accustomed to our crutches, isn't it? I broke the screen on my phone once and just never got it fixed. You get used to things. In the case of the invalid, what he was "used to" was a two-by-four-foot mat. The invalid's world consisted of eight square feet. He went through the same routine day after day after day. And while that might seem monotonous to us, it was also safe.

One man's mat is another man's security blanket. But if you want to get well, you can't keep sitting on it. You can't keep doing the same thing, going to the same places, or hanging with the same people. You've got to get rid of your mat—roll it up and toss it out. Or dump it. Or unfollow it. Or whatever else you need to do to remove yourself from something that is getting between you and Jesus.

Do you want to get well?

This question digs deep. For the invalid, getting well meant getting a job. It meant actually using his healed legs. It meant a new level of responsibility to society. Like every blessing from God, getting well comes with the burden of responsibility.

Tough Love

Sometimes we need someone to silly-slap us. It might injure our ego, but sometimes it gets the job done. I'm talking about a loving slap here, not an excuse to go ripping on everyone about everything.

That's exactly what a twenty-two-year-old intern did with me (Mark) when I was a young pastor. He confronted the pride he detected. Part of me wanted to quickly point out what was wrong with him! How dare an intern come at me! The problem was, he was right. I didn't like it when he said it, but I look back on that awkward moment as worth every ounce of awkwardness. And I have the utmost respect for that intern and everyone else who's had the courage to challenge me over the years.

The best friends ask the toughest questions. And by tough questions, I mean tough *love*. In the words of Proverbs 27:6, "Faithful are the wounds of a friend; profuse are the kisses of an enemy" (ESV). Don't surround yourself with people who kiss up or suck up. You need some people in your life who will get in your face! Not too many, but they should still be there.

Do you want to get well?

If you do, then you need to hear what you don't want to hear and do what you don't want to do. You can't expect God to do the supernatural if you aren't even willing to do the natural. You've got to do your part so God can do His part. Like the invalid, you've got to be willing to carry your weight. Only God can perform miracles, but there's almost always a human element involved.

Remember, Naaman had to dip in the Jordan River seven times.[3] The woman with the issue of blood had to fight through the crowds to get close enough to Jesus to touch the hem of His garment.[4] And the disciples had to haul in their nets and cast them on the other side of the boat.[5]

Some miracles take tough love.

Some miracles take time.

Some miracles take extra effort.

Some miracles take blood, sweat, and tears.

Atrophy

During my (Mark's) college basketball career, I had reconstructive surgery for a torn ACL in both of my knees. The most painful moment was getting out of bed for the first time after surgery. Have you ever had blood rush to one of your extremities after it's been elevated or the circulation has been cut off? The pain was so acute I almost passed out. Now imagine the invalid standing to his feet after thirty-eight years of being off of them.

Blood rush.

While the ligament graft in my knee healed in a matter of months, it took me much longer to regain the muscles that had atrophied. If you've ever played sports, you know what I'm talking about. It takes ages to build muscle, but no time at all to lose it. I actually wore an electrical stimulation device post-surgery to elicit muscle contractions via electrical impulses. Obviously, the invalid didn't have one of those! His legs were skin and bones. There was no muscle there. Even worse, he had no muscle memory. His mind didn't remember *how* to walk.

We take walking for granted, but it's quite the neuromusculoskeletal feat. Look around. We're the only truly bipedal creatures. Simply standing still requires marvelous coordination between highly sophisticated sensory systems—the small structures in the inner ear regulate balance, the proprioceptors in the joints detect small shifts in alignment, and our eyes provide visual information about the body's orientation in space.[6] So standing still is no simple feat, but ambulation (aka walking) is even more amazing.

When you walk, you function as an inverted pendulum. The kinetic energy of motion (that's Mass x Velocity^2 ÷ 2) is transformed into gravitational potential energy (Mass x Gravity x Height). If you were a perfect pendulum, you'd convert kinetic energy into potential energy and back without wasting a calorie. But we're only 65 percent of a perfect pendulum, which means that 35 percent of the energy for each step is supplied by the calories we burn. Birds and fish are way more efficient, even though they do stuff like fly and swim. In a lot of ways, walking is way more miraculous than flying or swimming, especially if you haven't done it in thirty-eight years! In my humble opinion, the invalid walking on land is no less miraculous than Jesus walking on water.

The Law of Requisite Variety

When Jesus told the invalid to get up and walk, He was asking him to do something he hadn't done in thirty-eight years. And that's what it takes if you want to experience the miraculous. You can't keep doing what you've always done! In fact, you might have to do something you haven't done in a long, long time! And don't use "I can't" as an excuse.

One way to change up an equation is to add or subtract something. You know this. It's also true with life. You have to do something less, do something more, or do something different. Easy math.

According to the law of requisite variety, the survival of any system depends on its capacity to cultivate variety in its internal structures. In other words, you have to keep changing. Perpetually staying the same dulls our senses, numbs our minds, and atrophies our muscles. Your world gets smaller and smaller until your universe is, well, about eight square feet.

If you know anything about exercise, you know routines eventually become bad news. If you exercise the same muscles the same way every time, your muscles start adapting and stop growing. The benefit just . . . leaves. What you need to do is throw them off. The same is true spiritually.

Routine is one key to spiritual growth. You might call it *spiritual disciplines* or just *good habits*. But when the routine becomes just routine, you have to change the routine. If you want to get out of a spiritual slump, you've gotta change something up.

Roll over to the homeless shelter.

Keep a gratitude journal.

Get outta town.

Try a new translation of the Bible.

Do a ten-day Daniel fast.[7]

Small changes in routine can make a radical difference. All you have to do is get to step one. The first step is always the longest and hardest, but after that . . . cake.

Self-Fulfilling Prophecies

The fact that the invalid is called *invalid* is kind of indicative. It'd be like if everyone called me *asthmatic*. This whole your-title-is-your-name deal is all over the place in the Bible—the prostitute with the alabaster jar, the man born blind, and the woman caught in the act of adultery, to name a few. They're synonymous with their sin. But there's a lesson here: *don't let what's wrong with you define you.* That's not who you are. When my kids lie to me, I don't call them liars. I remind them that that's not who they are. I don't let what they've done wrong define them.

We love to reduce people to labels in American culture. It's dehumanizing. Don't let anyone label you besides the One who made you. Take your cues from Scripture.

You are *more than a conqueror.*[8]

You are *the apple of God's eye.*[9]

You are *sought after.*[10]

You are *a joint heir with Christ.*[11]

You are *a child of God.*[12]

If you look up *impetuous* in the dictionary, there should be a picture of Peter. He was so dang unreliable! But Jesus gives him a new label—"The Rock."[13] You sure, Jesus? Nothing could have been further from the truth, but Jesus redefines Peter's identity and forecasts his future with one new label. Peter ultimately lived up to his new name.

Our words are far more powerful than we realize.

In 1963, Hall of Fame baseball pitcher Gaylord Perry made an offhanded comment before stepping into the batter's box: "They'll put a man on the moon before I hit a home run." It's true, most pitchers aren't great hitters. But it's rather ironic that Gaylord Perry hit the first and only home run of his baseball career six years later on July 20, 1969—just a few hours after Neil Armstrong set foot on the moon! Another version of this baseball legend attributes that statement to Perry's manager, Alvin Dark.[14] Either way, it illustrates a powerful principle that is true in every sphere of life, from athletics to economics. For better or for worse, our words are self-fulfilling prophecies. Negative prophecies are validated by fear. Positive prophecies are validated by faith.

When Jim Carrey was a struggling actor in his early days, he would drive up Mulholland Drive through the Santa Monica Mountains to a spot that overlooked the city of LA. Then he'd give himself a little pep talk: "Everybody wants to work with me. I'm a really good actor. I have all kinds of great movie offers." If you know anything about Jim Carrey, it's easy to imagine him doing that, isn't it? He later recalled, "I'd just repeat those things over and over, literally convincing myself that I had a couple movies lined up. Then I'd drive back down, ready to take on the world." Carrey wrote himself a check for 10 million bucks, postdated it for Thanksgiving of 1995, and wrote "For services rendered" on the memo line. Then he tucked that check into his wallet to remind himself of his dream every time he opened it. By the time Thanksgiving of 1995 rolled around, Jim Carrey's asking price was $20 million per movie.[15]

I'm not saying you can speak whatever you want into existence with your words. God can, but you're not Him. Then again, if your words line up with the Word of God, miracles tend to happen. You'll say what Jesus said and do what Jesus did. And that's precisely what Peter did. He witnessed the invalid being healed and followed suit not long after. On his way to the temple one day, Peter encountered a man who was lame from birth, sitting at the gate called Beautiful. Peter looked him in the eye and said, "Silver or gold I do not have, but what I do have I give you. In the name of Jesus Christ of Nazareth, walk."[16] And just like that, the lame man jumped for joy. So let me double back to *the* question: *Do you want to get well?*

If you don't, keep doing what you're doing.

If you do, take a step of faith. Then another. And another. And if you keep putting one foot in front of the other, you'll eventually get where God wants you to go. Most miracles are the by-product of "a long obedience in the same direction."[17] You can't just pick up your mat. You have to actually *walk*. But while you're walking, enjoy the journey.

THE
FOURTH
SIGN

Some time after this, Jesus crossed to the far shore of the Sea of Galilee (that is, the Sea of Tiberias), and a great crowd of people followed him because they saw the signs he had performed by healing the sick. Then Jesus went up on a mountainside and sat down with his disciples. The Jewish Passover Festival was near.

When Jesus looked up and saw a great crowd coming toward him, he said to Philip, "Where shall we buy bread for these people to eat?" He asked this only to test him, for he already had in mind what he was going to do.

Philip answered him, "It would take more than half a year's wages to buy enough bread for each one to have a bite!"

Another of his disciples, Andrew, Simon Peter's brother, spoke up, "Here is a boy with five small barley loaves and two small fish, but how far will they go among so many?"

Jesus said, "Have the people sit down." There was plenty of grass in that place, and they sat down (about five thousand men were there). Jesus then took the loaves, gave thanks, and distributed to those who were seated as much as they wanted. He did the same with the fish.

When they had all had enough to eat, he said to his disciples, "Gather the pieces that are left over. Let nothing be wasted." So they gathered them and filled twelve baskets with the pieces of the five barley loaves left over by those who had eaten.

John 6:1–13

Two Fish

Here is a boy with five small barley loaves and two
small fish, but how far will they go among so many?

John 6:9

Filet mignon with a blue cheese crust, extra butter sauce.

On special occasions Lora and I (Mark) visit heaven on earth:
Ruth's Chris Steak House. It's a food pilgrimage. I start eating
strategically twenty-four hours in advance to maximize the meal. I
stretch my stomach and eat tons of veggies so that first bite is even
more magical. I start salivating several hours prior to the reservation
(just at the thought of the reservation, not even the meal). When
the waiter sets that sizzling steak on the table, I feel like I'm at the
marriage supper of the Lamb. I imagine angels' voices sound like
that little *tttssss* of a Ruth's Chris steak. I worship God with every
bite. By the time dessert rolls around, revival's about to bust out.

Good food is one of God's most gracious gifts. Another one
of my personal favorites is Lou Malnati's pizza. If you want to

bribe me, send a four-pack of deep-dish pepperoni via UPS. One of the greatest moments of my life, right after watching my wife walk down the aisle on our wedding day and the birth of our three children, was making my very own pizza in Lou Malnati's kitchen at the invitation of their COO. No, I really am serious. Several times a year, we ship Malnati's from Chicago because I haven't convinced them yet to open one in DC.

Here's where I'm vulnerable: I can be a little possessive when it comes to Malnati's pizza. When our kids were younger, Lora and I would eat the Malnati's, but we'd put a regular store-bought pizza in the oven for our kids. Cruel? No, they just weren't ready. They hadn't reached the age of accountability yet, and I was afraid they wouldn't be mature enough to truly understand it.

All of that to say this: if I share my Malnati's with you, *I love you. A lot.*

Hold that thought.

The focal point of the fourth miracle is Jesus feeding the five thousand with five loaves and two fish. Actually, whoever started calling it the feeding of the five thousand shortchanged Jesus. There were five thousand *men.* So the grand total was probably closer to twenty thousand (that's men, women, and children). Jesus doesn't just pull a rabbit out of a hat here—He basically pulls out 19,998 fish. But that's the focal point. Let's talk about the appetizer, if you will.

The Pre-Miracle

Let's assume the disciples didn't steal this little guy's brown bag lunch. This boy gave it willingly. Then it was as much an expression of love as me sharing my Malnati's. Perhaps even more! It was also the pre-miracle that set up the miracle.

Getting kids to share anything takes a minor miracle! Their favorite word is *mine,* and they use it about everything, including what's yours. Getting them to share something they *love*, like their favorite food? That's a major miracle, right there.

This one act of sacrificial giving was the catalyst for one of Jesus' most amazing miracles. I know I say that about most miracles, but if they made the Bible, they must be one of His most amazing. Anyway, for the record, I don't see it as *one* miracle. It looks more like twenty thousand separate miracles.

If this boy didn't share his five loaves and two fish, there's nothing for Jesus to multiply. Am I suggesting Jesus could not have performed this miracle without the little boy's lunch? Yes and no. He could've easily materialized Malnati's for everybody. (But then the disciples might have just died right then and there.) The moral of the story: God doesn't do the supernatural if we don't pull our weight in the natural.

The lesson is so simple: if you put what you have in your hands into God's hands, He can make a lot out of a little!

In the natural world, it's easy to think that if you *give more*, you'll *have less*. But that's not how it works in God's economy. Things don't usually add up the normal way with Jesus. They tend to *multiply* exponentially: in God's economy, 5 + 2 doesn't equal 7. When you add God to the equation, 5 loaves + 2 fish = 5,000 meals with 12 to-go bags left over!

Run the Numbers

The total population of the Galilee region was close to forty thousand during this time. So, basically, half of them crossed the Sea of Galilee by boat or hiked by foot to get to the mountainside where Jesus had set up camp. When Scripture says Jesus "saw a great crowd coming toward him,"[1] it's no understatement. He probably heard and smelled them too.

It only makes sense that He would ask Philip how to feed the people, because Philip was from Bethsaida, nine miles away. If anyone knew the local joints, it would be Philip. But there wasn't a Panera around the corner. And even if there was, He knew they couldn't afford to feed everyone.

Philip's response borders on rude: "It would take more than half a year's wages to buy enough bread for each one to have a bite!"[2]

Translation: *Bethsaida, we have a problem!* At face value this situation looks like a logistical and financial nightmare.

Philip wasn't the money man, but it didn't take Judas to figure out that this lunch would break the bank. Just hiring the wait-staff would have set them back thousands. And even if everyone ordered off the dollar menu, the meal would have cost tens of thousands.

What do you do when the will of God doesn't add up?

In my experience, the will of God rarely "adds up." By definition, a God-sized dream is going to be *beyond your resources and your ability*. In other words, you can't afford it and you can't accomplish it. Not in your lifetime! But God can do more in *one day* than you can accomplish in a hundred lifetimes. He owns the cattle on a thousand hills.[3] The twenty thousand covered *one* hill, and one person certainly doesn't eat a whole cow. The point is: He could have fed a lot more.

Your job is *not* to crunch numbers on the will of God. When you add God to the equation, His output always exceeds your input. And your two fish can go a lot further than you'd imagine if you just hand 'em over.

Enough Isn't Enough

Few people have witnessed more miracles than George Müller.

Along with pastoring one church for sixty-six years, Müller established the Ashley Down orphanage in Bristol, England. He cared for 10,024 orphans while establishing 117 schools for their education throughout England. Adjusted for inflation, George

Müller raised $150 million. That's an incredible sum of money by any standard, but what makes it even more remarkable is the fact that George Müller never asked anyone for anything—not a single penny. He decided to ask *only God*. Müller figured that God knew exactly what he needed and when he needed it, and God could make provision for it. It's estimated that Müller experienced thirty thousand specific answers to prayer, as recorded in his journal. Time and time again, food was dropped off on his family's doorstep right when they ran out, a donation was made right before a bill came due, or a plumber offered his services right when a problem needed to be fixed.

I live by an Oswald Chambers maxim: "Let God be as original with other people as he is with you."[4] So I'm not saying that we should all make like George Müller. I really do think it's okay to ask for help—but shouldn't we put it to prayer *first* rather than last? Why do we take matters into our own hands when we can put them into the hands of God? Few things are harder than *letting go and letting God*, but that's what Mr. Müller modeled. After all, he had thirty thousand reasons why God's the answer.

Remember the Lord's Prayer? "Give us this day our daily bread."[5]

What I really wish is that it said *weekly* or *monthly* or *yearly* bread. That way I wouldn't have to depend on Him on a daily basis! Spiritual maturity is not self-sufficiency. In fact, our desire for self-sufficiency is a subtle expression of our sinful nature. Really, the more mature you are, the more needy you get! You start depending on God for everything. We desire to get to a place where we don't need God. We want God to make us not need God so much. And that brings us full circle: everyone wants a miracle, but no one wants to be in a situation that necessitates one. But one way or another, we usually end up in situations where *enough isn't enough*. All of a sudden, someone has to feed twenty thousand people, and all we've got is two fish and some graham crackers.

Ring the Bell

I'm not sure what the dinner ritual looks like at your house, but we call our kids to the dinner table when the food is almost ready for annihilation. Then I pray a short prayer, because it's just bad stewardship to miss having a meal while it's hot.

Never once have I called the kids to an empty table. It accentuates the absurdity of the fourth miracle. Jesus says:

Have the people sit down.[6]

Jesus rings the dinner bell, but the table's empty! He has everybody take a seat, as if they're going to eat. He even blesses the imaginary meal. But as it stands, He's going to have to split two fish twenty thousand ways.

Have you ever had to wait for a meal longer than expected? Or had a waiter tell you they ran out of whatever you ordered?

The longer I have to wait, the hungrier and grumpier I get. It can get ugly fast. And anyone who's worked in food service knows what I'm talking about. This may not seem like a dangerous situation, but if dinner isn't served, this crowd of twenty thousand turns into a mob.

That's why this prayer ranks as one of Jesus' most amazing. He's so calm and collected. He's like the perfect waiter! John doesn't reference Jesus' prayer, but the other Gospels do, and it's the same prayer He prays at the Last Supper. In both instances, I'm not sure that my words would have been dripping with gratitude. But Jesus gives thanks.

Jesus thanks His Father for something He doesn't have.
Jesus thanks His Father for something that hasn't happened yet.

Don't wait until *after* God does the miracle to give thanks. Give thanks *before*. Nothing sets us up for a miracle like giving thanks.

Count the Fish

So they gathered them and filled twelve baskets with
the pieces of the five barley loaves left over by those
who had eaten.

John 6:13

My friend Joel Clark is an author and filmmaker. Along with being
off-the-charts creative, Joel is also one of the most compassionate
people I know. Much of his film work has focused on documenting
the suffering of those who don't live in the land of opportunity.
But Joel wasn't always that way.

For nearly a decade, Joel served on staff at a church in South
Africa. But his relationship with God had become a little more
professional than personal. He was low on money and even lower
on morale. His heart was hardening right along with his spiritual
hearing. But that dramatically changed during a late-night McDonald's run. The 38 rand in his pocket was just enough to indulge
himself in a Happy Meal (a rand is like a nickel to us). Joel was so

focused on his own issues that he barely noticed the street kids in the parking lot. For the first time in quite a while, Joel heard that still small voice of the Holy Spirit: *Buy those kids some hamburgers.* Joel had a decision to make: order a Happy Meal for himself or buy burgers for those street kids. He didn't have enough money to do both. "I was filled with bitterness and pettiness," Joel said. "Even though I ordered five junior cheeseburgers for those kids, I didn't do it with the right attitude." But despite Joel's doing the right thing with the wrong attitude, God still showed up and showed off.

When Joel walked out the door of McDonald's, the group of street kids had doubled. Joel contemplated cutting the burgers in half so everyone could have one. But when he started handing them out, they multiplied like the Filet-O-Fish that fed five thousand. Did McDonald's give him the wrong order? Did they throw in extras because it was closing time? Or did God reach into His bag of tricks and pull out some junior cheeseburgers? Joel has no idea to this day, but when he had given a burger to every street kid, he found one extra at the bottom of the bag for himself.

Joel calls it his McMoment. The lesson wasn't lost on him: if you give your Happy Meal to Jesus, it'll go a lot further in His hands than it would in your stomach.

If you keep giving, God will keep multiplying. But you have to trust God enough to obey Him in the little things.

Lord Algebra

Up until the sixteenth century, mathematics had two subfields: arithmetic and geometry. Then the French mathematician François Viète pioneered a new field called algebra. In doing so, he single-handedly bombed the SAT scores of the mathematically challenged and probably kept you out of the college you wanted to get into.

Advanced Algebra ranks as one of my all-time least favorite classes, right before Trigonometry and right after Calculus. I didn't get it then, and I still don't get it now. But it helps me appreciate one of the hats Jesus wore: teacher. He didn't just teach religion. I guess in some ways, He also taught math. That has to be the hardest subject to teach.

Jesus was so brilliant at designing tests that half the time His disciples didn't even know they were taking them! Philip is a good example:

> [Jesus] asked this only to test him, for he already had in mind what he was going to do.[1]

The disciples had already failed Algebra I.

When Jesus fed the four thousand with seven loaves, it should've given them the faith to believe that He could feed five thousand with five loaves![2] But as usual, they're lost. Do you ever look at a test and just . . . blank? Everything leaves you? That's the disciples every day. They act like it's their first day in class. So Jesus graciously gives them a makeup test.

If the first miracle reveals that nothing's too small for God, the fourth miracle counterbalances it: *nothing is too big for God.*

When the little boy offered to share his lunch, Andrew's reaction was, "Thanks, but no thanks!" He didn't think it would make a difference: "How far will they go among so many?"[3] But Andrew was overanalyzing the situation, like most of us, and he almost missed the miracle because of it.

The boy with the lunch could have been pretty dumb and still known that 2 + 2 = 4. He knew his two fish weren't enough to make a dent. It was a drop in the bucket. But he didn't let what he *didn't have* keep him from giving what he *did have* to Jesus. And that's the precursor to tons of miracles! I hope I'm really drilling that in.

Like so many unsung heroes in the Bible, this little boy walks off the pages of Scripture never to be heard of again. But his fifteen minutes of fame have stretched into two thousand years. I wouldn't be surprised if he's the seafood chef in heaven.

Seven and a Half Feet

This book revolves around the seven miracles in John's Gospel (hopefully you've figured that out), but I have a confession to make. There is an eighth miracle, the miraculous catch of fish, tucked away in the back of John's book.[4] It's like a little bonus miracle—like that extra scene after the credits in Marvel movies.

I (Mark) don't know the first thing about fishing. That's a sad truth given the fact that I was born in Minnesota, the land of ten thousand lakes. Our family vacationed on one of them, Lake Ida, every year until I turned twenty-one. Every year we had a friendly little fishing contest, which I never won. My brother Don is the fish whisperer in our family. The fish would just feast on his lures. My lures (usually the exact same ones) must have been fish-repelling.

So I know next to nothing about fishing, but there's one thing I know for sure: fishermen count fish. They measure their weight and length. They most definitely tally their total catch. That's why the specificity of the eighth miracle doesn't surprise me at all. I'm guessing they actually counted two or three times to cross-check the exact number. I'm not sure what an average fishing trip would net, but they'd been fishing all night with zero luck. Nothin'. The fish simply weren't biting. Then Jesus told them to fish on the other side of the boat. Let's zoom out right there.

First-century fishing boats were seven and a half feet wide.

So what's the point of trying the other side?

What difference does ninety inches make?

Jesus illustrates it best: sometimes ninety inches is the difference between 0 and 153. You might literally (even at this moment) be seven and a half feet from a miracle—but you have to try the other side!

Miracles don't just happen when we believe God for big things. Miracles happen when we obey God in the little things. When we do little things like they're big things, God will do big things like they're little things.

I love that Jesus is always using fish in His miracles, because that's definitely the one area where the disciples might have been tempted to assert superiority. I wonder if they honestly believed that they knew a thing or two about fishing that Jesus didn't. I mean, Jesus was a carpenter. They were practically born in a fishing boat. This was their domain. This was their strong suit. And that's usually where it's hardest to trust God. We start trusting in our God-given gifts instead of the God who gave them to us in the first place.

Lord Ichthyoid

Throughout history, some of the church's most brilliant scholars have speculated on the significance of the number 153. Jerome referenced Oppian's *Halieutica*, which cited exactly 153 species of fish in the Sea of Galilee. Augustine of Hippo noted that 153 is the sum of the first 17 integers, making it a triangular number. He also claimed that 17 is the perfect combination of law and grace: the Ten Commandments plus 7 gifts of the Spirit. Evagrius Ponticus further expounded on the mathematical properties of 153 by noting that 100 is a square number, 28 is a triangular number, and 25 is a circular number. Weird stuff.

To be candid, I don't think the number 153 was included for the sake of symbolism. I mean, if there are 153 species of fish in the Sea of Galilee and the disciples caught one of each, Jesus gets major style points. But that's not the point. Its specificity is setting an example: measure the miracle carefully. "Count the fish" is shorthand for "measure the miracle."

Yes, miracles are mysterious. Not every miracle can be quantified, but the ones that can be, should be. Right? Isn't that why Jesus sent the lepers to see the priest? He wanted the miracle to be validated. If MRIs were around then, the before and after pictures of some of Jesus' miracles would be ridiculous. We need to measure our miracles with X-rays, dollars, facts, numbers, tests, and pictures. Count the miracle like you count blessings.

When Jesus told the disciples to try the other side of the boat, they could've gotten all offended. "Don't tell us how to do our job. We know this sea better than You do. We're the ones who've been fishing all night." And if they had taken offense, they would have missed the miracle.

What do you do when God's logic doesn't line up with yours? When the will of God doesn't add up? What about when you think you know better than God?

Just look at Peter the first time Jesus multiplied a catch of fish:

Master, we've worked hard all night and haven't caught anything. But because you say so, I will let down the nets.[5]

Peter took Him at His word: "*Because you say so.*"

God said it. I believe it. That settles it. Of course, you might have to take a ninety-inch step of faith as well.

Are you willing to try the other side of the boat?

THE FIFTH SIGN

When evening came, his disciples went down to the lake, where they got into a boat and set off across the lake for Capernaum. By now it was dark, and Jesus had not yet joined them. A strong wind was blowing and the waters grew rough. When they had rowed about three or four miles, they saw Jesus approaching the boat, walking on the water; and they were frightened. But he said to them, "It is I; don't be afraid." Then they were willing to take him into the boat, and immediately the boat reached the shore where they were heading.

John 6:16–21

12

The Water Walker

When they had rowed about three or four miles, they
saw Jesus walking on the sea.

John 6:19 ESV

Ever wonder why the capital of the United States is located in
Washington, DC? A swamp? There's a miracle behind it. I first
heard this little-known legend from a congressman during a late-
night tour of the Capitol building, but firsthand witnesses and
secondhand evidence show it's legit.

On August 24, 1814, a British force of four thousand led by
General Robert Ross marched into Washington, DC. Most of the
eight thousand residents had already evacuated the city, including
First Lady Dolly Madison, who managed to salvage the Declara-
tion of Independence and Gilbert Stuart's full-length portrait of
President George Washington.

The British began the systematic burning of the Treasury Building, the Capitol, and the President's Palace, which was renamed the White House after it was whitewashed to cover up smoke damage from the fire. One of the few buildings left standing was the Marine Barracks at 8th and I (literally across the street from our Capitol Hill church campus).

Tradition has it that the British left the barracks unburned out of reverence for the Marine Corps, who stayed to fight. Truth be told, they probably just needed a place to bunk that night. Fun fact: one of the few surviving buildings, a four-story brick brownstone between the Marine Barracks and the Navy Yard, is now owned by National Community Church. It may be the oldest commercial building on Capitol Hill, predating the invasion of Washington by nearly a decade.

With much of the city in ashes, pretty much everybody wanted to move the capital from Washington back to Philadelphia where the First Continental Congress met, but the bill to relocate the capital was voted down by Congress. The swing vote was a miracle that our Founding Fathers attributed to the providence of God.

According to the *Old Farmer's Almanac*, temperatures on August 24, 1814, soared above 100 degrees Fahrenheit. As the British set fire to government buildings, there was no reprieve in sight. But out of nowhere, a furious thunderstorm arrived on the scene unexpected and unannounced. Like a heavenly sprinkler system, the heavy rains kept the White House from completely burning flat.

The severe windstorm that followed spooked the British as it blew over cannons and caused barrels of gunpowder to spontaneously combust. The weather alone may not be the reason British troops withdrew, but many Redcoats believed it was a sign from God. And many members of Congress who voted to keep the capital in Washington concurred. They believed it was a sign from God, like one straight outta the book of John.

Seventy-Minute Miracle

I (Mark) once took a class in meteorology at the University of Chicago, and thus began my love affair with the weather. One of my favorite things to do on vacation is to watch the weather channel, which my family has great fun with. By fun, of course, I mean they make fun of me.

Two thousand years ago, predicting the weather was a crap-shoot. A few aphorisms were everyone's best guess: "Red sky at night, sailor's delight. Red sky in morning, sailor take warning." Of course, even with the aid of weather satellites, our best forecasts still feel like a fifty-fifty coin flip. We might understand Mother Nature a little better now, but she's still as unpredictable as ever.

We use reinforced concrete to protect ourselves against earthquakes and storm shutters to safeguard against hurricanes, but we still can't do much about the weather. All we can do is talk about it when there's nothing else to talk about. But there *is* One who commands the wind and waves. The One who turned water into wine also turned the Sea of Galilee into glass: "Peace, be still!"[1] Three words is all it takes.

The Sea of Galilee is the setting for a bunch of Jesus' miracles. Some of them happen below the surface of the water, like 153 fish spontaneously deciding to swim all together under one boat in the middle of a huge lake. Others happen *above* the surface, like stopping a tropical storm in its tracks. But the most astonishing may be the fifth miracle in John's Gospel. This isn't just a stroll across the pond. The Water Walker covered at least three and a half miles! At an average walking pace of three miles per hour, this miracle most likely lasted at least seventy minutes.

The density of water is one gram per cubic centimeter at 4 degrees Celsius. Translation: humans sink in water. The surface tension of water can support the superhydrophobic water strider, also known as the pond skater. Then there's the infamous Jesus Christ lizard, star of many a YouTube video. But that's pretty much it. (And the Basilisk lizard cheats. But that's another story.) When it comes to the human species, we're not well equipped for water walking. If you could sprint 67 mph, then you could actually run on water, but the fastest recorded foot speed is 27.79 mph by Jamaican Olympic gold medalist Usain Bolt. Reaching 67 mph would require fifteen times more energy than the human body is capable of expending.[2]

Surfing the Sea of Galilee

In April 2006, *The Journal of Paleolimnology* published a paper with the dubious title: "Is There a Paleolimnological Explanation for 'Walking on Water' in the Sea of Galilee?" An expert in oceanography and limnology, Dr. Doron Nof, and his coauthors assert that an odd combination of atmospheric conditions may cause rare patches of floating ice on the Sea of Galilee. According to their calculations, the chances of this floating ice phenomenon happening are less than once every thousand years. But those odds didn't deter them from questioning whether Jesus walked on water after all. Perhaps Jesus just surfed a patch of floating ice.[3]

To be honest, I'm not sure which one would be more amazing. Surfing across the Sea of Galilee on a piece of floating ice that only rolls around once every couple thousand years would take miraculous balance and timing. I'd love to see an HD, slow-motion instant replay of either one—walking on water or surfing on ice. In my opinion, this hypothesis reveals a lot about human nature: we just have a natural tendency to explain away what we don't get. That's why most of us miss the miracle. Remember the old aphorism, "You have to see it to believe it"? It's true, but the opposite is even truer: *you have to believe it to see it.*

The brain has limits. Especially the left side. Stuff like this just doesn't compute—there is no cognitive category for supernatural. Like a small calculator that can't go past a couple digits, miracles just register as an intellectual error. That's why the disciples didn't recognize Jesus at first. They thought He was a ghost, which isn't a logical reaction either.

Nine Dolphins

If you don't know TED, go to TED.com right now. One of my favorite TED talks is by Al Seckel, an expert on visual perception and sensory illusion.[4] During the lecture, he shows the audience a stenciled drawing that they readily recognize as a couple intimately embracing. But when that same image is shown to children, they cannot see the couple. Seckel explains that the children can't see it simply because they don't have a prior memory to associate with the picture. In other words, they have no cognitive category for what they're seeing. For what it's worth, most children say they see nine dolphins.

The reason many of us miss the miracles that are all around us all the time is because we don't have a prior memory to associate with them. That's why the disciples thought Jesus was a ghost. I guess it made more sense than someone actually walking on water.

Imagination is a function of memory. You can only really draw from what you've experienced—what you've seen or heard or felt. Ideas don't materialize out of thin air (unless of course it's an idea from God via the Holy Spirit). But the boundary line around imagination is drawn by past experience. New experiences and new ideas expand our borders.

In his book *Mozart's Brain and the Fighter Pilot*, Richard Restak shares a profound truism: learn more, see more. He notes, "The richer my knowledge of flora and fauna of the woods, the more I'll be able to see. Our perceptions take on richness and depth as a result of all the things that we learn. What the eye sees is determined by what the brain has learned."[5]

When astronomers look into the night sky, they have a greater appreciation than others for the constellations and stars and planets. They see more because they know more. When musicians listen to a symphony, they have a greater appreciation for the chords and melodies and instrumentation. They hear more because they know more. When sommeliers sample a wine, they have a greater appreciation for the flavor, texture, and origin. They literally taste more because they know more.

Great love is born of great knowledge. And the more you know, the more you know how much you don't know. True knowledge doesn't puff up; it just makes you want to worship more and more and more and more.

It also beckons us out of the boat.

Embrace the Mystery

How do you react to something brand new—something you have *zero* experience to associate it with? What do you do when God does freaky, "unrealistic" stuff? What happens when Jesus shows up in the least likely way at the least likely time in the least likely place?

One option is to ignore the miracles. Be like a little kid playing peekaboo and cover your eyes. Another option is disbelief. You can reject them altogether, a la Thomas Jefferson. The new thing to do is to intellectualize miracles, but our attempts to outsmart the Omniscient One make us sound awfully silly. My advice? Don't even bother. Embrace the mystery of the miracle! No sense in trying to explain it. The miracles of God make us appreciate the mystery of God. They also help us see God for who He is—the Wine Maker, the Water Walker, the Grave Robber, and so on and so on.

God's more than a subject to be studied.

He is the *object* of all wonder. Cool, yeah?

Second Timothy 2:15 tells us to study and show ourselves

approved. But *systematic theology* is the ultimate oxymoron. It's like *white bread*. It's not a thing. God defies definition. He can be known-ish, but never fully known. Again, the more you know, the more you know how much you don't know. The net result of seeking God isn't just knowledge. It's mystery. To be honest, anything less than mystery is idolatry. Why? It's a psychological projection—it's a human attempt to create God in our image. But what you end up with is a dumbed-down version of the gospel.

When it comes to lining up reality and theology, we go the wrong way: we try to fit theology into reality. Doubt is downgrading your theology to match your experience of reality. Faith is the exact opposite. Instead of allowing circumstances to get between you and God, faith is putting God between you and your circumstances. It's not *denying* reality. It's recognizing that there's a reality that is more real than what you can perceive with your five senses. Faith is a sixth sense that enables us to perceive the impossible. Cool stuff, really.

One of my all-time favorite quotes is a Mark Nepo classic: "Birds don't need ornithologists to fly."[6] Well, water walkers don't need limnologists to walk on water! If you follow in the footsteps of Jesus long enough, you'll eventually walk on water. You'll go impossible places and do unimaginable things. Water walking becomes a way of life.

Boldly Go

When I was a kid, there was a television show called *Star Trek*—the original—and the opening narration at the beginning of every episode was just unforgettable:

> Space: the final frontier. These are the voyages of the starship *Enterprise*. Its five-year mission: to explore strange new worlds, to seek out new life and new civilizations, to boldly go where no man has gone before.[7]

I quote that last line, "to boldly go where no man has gone before," all the time. It's awesome. And for some reason, I think of it every time I read this verse:

> The wind blows where it wishes, and you hear its sound, but you do not know where it comes from or where it goes. So it is with everyone who is born of the Spirit.[8]

Translation: God is awfully good at getting us where God wants us to go, but there will be some crazy twists and turns along the way! My friend Jeff Ellis recently shared one of those twists.

After visiting his daughter in DC, Jeff got stuck in Beltway traffic on the way to the airport and missed his flight. He was still irritated when he boarded the next available flight. Jeff found his seat and wanted nothing more than to mind his own business. That's when a very extroverted old man and his wife sat next to him. Jeff, who isn't chatty to begin with, knew it was going to be a very long flight.

Jeff happened to have a copy of *The Circle Maker*, and his seatmates noticed it. Turns out, the man and his wife had just attended the National Prayer Breakfast. And they'd missed their flight as well. Zing.

Then Jeff dropped the courtesy question, "What do you do?" During the ensuing conversation, the retired doctor told him that he was a friend of the CEO of Tyson Foods (the chicken nugget people), Donnie Smith. Then his wife mentioned that their daughter had adopted two girls from Ethiopia. When Jeff asked from where in Ethiopia, they told him it was a small village named Mekelle.

Jeff may as well have been shot with a *Star Trek* stun gun. Jeff's son, David, moved to Mekelle, Ethiopia, a few years earlier to start Mekelle Farms and Chicken Hatchery! In Jeff's words, "What are the odds of two people on the whole plane even knowing where Mekelle Farms is in Ethiopia, much less sitting together on a flight neither of them were scheduled to be on? And to think that the conversation started over a copy of *The Circle Maker*."

If your vision is to establish the poultry industry in Ethiopia, a meeting with the CEO of Tyson Foods doesn't hurt. The doctor made a phone call, and David had the opportunity to spend a couple hours with Donnie Smith soon thereafter in Rwanda. David's chicken farm now partners with one of Tyson's subsidiaries, hatching 150,000 chicks a month and counting.

Maybe you feel like you're on the wrong plane. Lemme remind you: God is *good* at getting us where He wants us to go, even when it's our fault for missing a flight. You may be one seat assignment or one phone call from a miracle!

13

Dare the Devil

A strong wind was blowing and the waters grew rough.

John 6:18

High-risk high-wire spectacles—who do you think of? Seven generations of Flying Wallendas have performed jaw-dropping feats of balance for kings and queens and millions of circus-going kids. The most famous Flying Wallenda, Karl, died at the age of seventy-three after falling from a high wire between high-rise hotels in Puerto Rico.

Karl's great-grandson, Nik Wallenda, is the latest and perhaps greatest aerialist ever. This man's got seven Guinness World Records under his belt already. Nik secured his place in the history books with the first tightrope crossing of Niagara Falls. The most meaningful stunt may be his re-creation of the Puerto Rico walk that claimed his great-grandfather's life. But his masterpiece is undoubtedly the unprecedented and unparalleled Grand Canyon crossing of June 22, 2013, which I watched live along with much of America. He crossed the canyon on a two-inch tightrope fifteen hundred feet above the canyon floor with no safety net.

It was Nik's grandfather who impressed upon him at an early age that safety nets give a false sense of security. Hmm, now there's a lesson.

I know it's been said a thousand times in a thousand ways. But like each of the secrets I've shared, it's easier said than done. Many of us fail to achieve our dreams or experience the miraculous because we're more focused on not falling than on setting records. There comes a moment when you need to quit preparing for the life you want to live and start living it.

When Lora and I (Mark) felt God calling us to the nation's capital, we got a U-Haul and moved to DC. We had no safety net—no family, no place to live, and no guaranteed salary. But we took a 595-mile step of faith because we believed that our destiny was DC. It felt like we were crossing a canyon, but we never looked down, never looked back.

More than thirteen million viewers from 217 countries watched the canyon crossing, breaking the Discovery Channel's ratings record. They also heard Nik praise Jesus for what seemed like the longest 22 minutes and 54 seconds in television history.

When you've been walking on wires since the age of two, risk becomes second nature. For Nik Wallenda, wire walking is a way of life. He doesn't evade danger; he seeks it. He's fearless, even suspended fifteen hundred feet above the Grand Canyon with thirty-mile-per-hour wind gusts.

To call Nik Wallenda a daredevil would be an obvious understatement. The guy's from a family who does human pyramids on high wires. But Nik doesn't get that daring streak just from his DNA.

Shock and Awe

Let's redefine *daredevil*. It's more than just risking of life and limb for no good reason. Etymologically (looking at the derivative of the word), it means *to dare the devil*. A defining characteristic of anyone who follows Christ should be daredevilry. The Son of God went forty rounds with the devil in the desert. Fearlessness is one of the most overlooked and underappreciated dimensions of His kaleidoscopic personality.

Jesus is the definition of *daredevil*.

I'd love to have seen the look in His eyes when the money changers were screaming like little children as He did some table-flippage with a homemade whip.[1] The most amazing part of this incident isn't even what Jesus did but what the temple guard *didn't* do. Why didn't this ancient SWAT team arrest Him? Shock and awe! What kind of daredevil would pull a stunt like that?

Only *the* Daredevil.

In the timeless words of Dorothy Sayers:

> The people who crucified Jesus never, to do them justice, accused him of being a bore—on the contrary, they thought him too dynamic to be safe. It has been left for later generations to muffle up that shattering personality and surround him with an atmosphere of tedium. We have very efficiently pared the claws of the Lion of Judah, certified him "meek and mild," and recommended him as a fitting household pet for pale curates and pious old ladies.[2]

Let's be honest: if Sayers's generation declawed the Lion of Judah, we neutered Him. Or at least lobotomized His wild side. And then we feel like faith is boring. Gee, I wonder why. We've given people just enough Jesus to be bored, but not enough to enthrall. He's the Lamb of God, but He's also the Lion of Judah.

Remember the showdown between Jesus and a demoniac named Legion?[3] Legion's nickname is a not-so-subtle reference to a Roman military division that consisted of as many as six thousand soldiers. It's no wonder this demon-possessed man couldn't be bound by chains—he had the strength of six thousand demons. And a man with a death wish is particularly dangerous—and the dude lived in a graveyard.

When Jesus docked in the region of the Gerasenes, Legion spotted Him from a distance and started running toward Him. Hit the Pause button right here. The Bible doesn't talk about the reaction of the disciples, but that's the part I wanna know! When Legion started running, I bet they did too. But Jesus doesn't flinch. Fearless in the face of evil.

The odds on this cage fight were 6,000 to 1, but Jesus still dares the devil. In boxing terms, it was a technical knockout—the demoniac fell to his knees before the opening bell. Then Jesus dunked the devil by casting that legion of demons into a herd of pigs that ran into the Sea of Galilee and drowned.

Fearlessness

John said it best:

> Perfect love casts out fear.[4]

Love is more than sappy stuff. Biblically speaking, it's synonymous with fearlessness.

If you fear God, there's just nothing else to fear. That includes death *and* all his friends. He has no license to violate your free will. The blood of Jesus is your shield, and the Word of God is your sword. Feel free to assert your authority as a child of the King anytime.

There are several thousand classified fears and phobias, but we're born with only two innate fears: the fear of falling and the fear of loud noises. Every other fear is learned, which means that every other fear can be unlearned. The fear of failure, the fear of people's opinions, the fear of the future . . . they're all bogus. A little of God's love magic and they're gone. If you keep growing in God's love, all that'll be left is the fear of God.

One of my prayers for my children is that they will have soft hearts and strong spines. I want their hearts to be sensitized to the still small voice of the Holy Spirit! I pray that their hearts would break for the things that break the heart of God, and to stand for what's right. We live in a culture where it's wrong to say something is wrong. Not only is that wrong, but it makes it even more ridiculously hard to do what's right. It takes a daredevil for that.

> We're not commissioned to hold the fort until Jesus returns.
>
> He commands us to invade enemy territory and reclaim it for righteousness.
>
> Jesus didn't suffer a brutal death on the cross just to keep us safe and sound.
>
> The goal was to make us dangerous.
>
> He died to make us daredevils.

Miracle by Moonlight

We often miss the juicy details that make Jesus' miracles so delicious, because we're two thousand years removed. However, in some spots, the Bible's pretty straightforward:

> A strong wind was blowing and the waters grew rough.[5]

Because of its low elevation, the Sea of Galilee has warmer air temperatures over it than surrounding areas. So it's not uncommon for sudden storms to sweep down the Jordan River valley. In March 1992, a storm brought in ten-foot waves that significantly damaged the modern city of Tiberias. The storm system described in John's Gospel may have produced waves that were half as high or twice as high, but one way or the other, it was *nasty*. Five- to twenty-foot waves is no one's idea of fun.

Let that register for a sec.

Have you ever experienced the crippling power of a wave?

I've been body-slammed while boogie boarding in the Atlantic a time or two . . . on three- to five-foot waves. Even a five-footer can knock the wind out of you or knock you clean out. I've done an ocean triathlon with seven-foot waves. Fighting the waves to reach the first buoy was far more difficult than crossing the finish line. I've spent twenty hours on the high seas island-hopping in the Galápagos. Our dinghy wasn't big enough for our mission team or for the billowing waves that caused all of us (except my intrepid, dauntless son) to lose our lunch.

I have a friend who works with a surfing school for aspiring professionals in Jeffreys Bay, South Africa. He recently told me about his first time big wave surfing in Cape Town. His idea of a big wave is so much bigger than what the rest of us think a "big" wave is. Building size. Twenty- to thirty-foot swells. To pull it off, he needed a towboard and heavy compression jacket. His friend Dougal, a big wave surfer who gave him the jacket, said it wouldn't keep him from drowning, but it would keep his intestines from exploding if he had to take a set on his head.

My point?

Jesus walked on this stuff.

I don't know about you, but when I'm stuck with a new challenge, I usually try to stack as many factors in my favor as possible. I want some failure insurance and a *guarantee* of success. I need the odds to be ever in my favor. So in this situation, I'd wait it out. Wait for sunrise, smooth water, and a cool breeze. That way, it's safer *and* everybody would see me do it.

Not Jesus.

Jesus did this miracle by moonlight because He wasn't looking for attention. It was the fourth watch of the night—right before dawn when it's darkest. That low visibility definitely increased the degree of difficulty, and I don't think the Daredevil would have had it any other way. Walking on water is impossible under any circumstances, but doing it in the middle of the night in rough waters is a little harder, a little scarier.

It's an easily overlooked detail, but why the heck were the disciples rowing across the Sea of Galilee in the middle of the night in the middle of a storm in the first place? They were following their Captain's orders—orders I probably would've second-guessed. They had crossed the same sea earlier that day, hiked up a mountainside, and waited on a dinner party of twenty thousand. Then Jesus asked them to work the night shift by rowing back across the Sea of Galilee. Nonstop for these guys. The disciples were at the end of their rope . . . and that's when you're getting close to a miracle.

Uncharted Waters

A block from Ebenezer's coffeehouse is a statue honoring one of our city's namesakes, Christopher Columbus. The inscription says: "To the memory of Christopher Columbus, whose high faith and indomitable courage gave to mankind a new world." Columbus and his crew would have never discovered the new world if they had not left the old world behind. The most amazing fact may be that prior to their history-changing voyage, not one of his crew members had ever been more than three hundred miles offshore.

In the words of Nobel Laureate André Gide, "One doesn't discover new lands without consenting to lose sight of the shore for a very long time."[6]

The Sea of Galilee is seven and a half miles wide and seventeen miles long, with a maximum depth of one hundred fifty-seven feet. John's Gospel specifically mentions that the disciples had rowed thirty furlongs, a little more than three and a half miles, out to sea.[7] The significance of that is this: they were nowhere near shore. Fortunately, that's where most miracles happen. They don't happen in the shallow end of the pool. They happen when you jump off the high dive into the deep end where you can't touch bottom.

That's what my friend Jack did when he moved to South Africa to do ministry serving surfers. God called and he went. All he had was a few dollars in his wallet and the change in his pocket—no safety net. He thought he was going to work with a ministry called

Surf Life, but God had very different plans for Jack. And that's what happens when you follow Jesus. You think you're going someplace to do something, but God often has an alternative itinerary you know nothing about. Lora and I didn't move to Washington, DC, to pastor National Community Church. It didn't even exist yet. We thought we were moving to DC to start a parachurch ministry, but God had a hidden agenda. He always does. He tells us to set sail for Capernaum, and we naturally think that is the objective. But you never know when or how or where Jesus might show up.

When Jack was twenty-six, he heard God's voice while smoking a joint on I-26 just outside Charleston, South Carolina. Now that's an unlikely circumstance. And I strongly discourage replicating those circumstances! But it does reveal God's ability to show up anywhere, anytime, anyhow. God told Jack that if he'd follow Him, He would use Jack's life to tell His story, and make a movie out of it. When Jack set sail for South Africa several years later, that promise was all but forgotten. Then Jesus entered stage right—walking on water.

Jack was hosting a large surfing outreach in Jeffreys Bay. That same day, a South African movie director named Bruce MacDonald and his production assistant were scouting out possible sets for a scene from their upcoming movie, *The Perfect Wave*. While he was driving, Bruce sensed a still small voice prompting him to turn down one of the side streets. Bruce had surfed almost every beach in Jeffreys Bay, but he'd never seen the beach at the end of this particular block.

When he pulled into the parking lot, Bruce got out of the car, walked straight up to Jack, and asked him who he was. Something clicked in both of their spirits. Bruce had declined ten different Hollywood-caliber actors who had auditioned for the costarring role opposite Clint Eastwood's son, Scott. In what must rank as one of the strangest auditions ever, Jack did a reading for the casting director on the spot, right in the parking lot, and got the role of the wild child. Honestly, Jack didn't have to do much acting because that's who Jack was. And just like the story line of his own life, the climax of the movie is redemption.

Most miracles don't happen within sight of the shoreline. You have to row about thirty furlongs out to sea. You have to venture into uncharted waters. And if you do, don't be shocked if God surprises you by showing up in the most unlikely places at the most unlikely times. You might even mistake God for a ghost, but that is the nature of God. The Water Walker loves waltzing into our lives at crazy times and places. That's how He shows up and shows off His power.

THE SIXTH SIGN

As he went along, he saw a man blind from birth. His disciples asked him, "Rabbi, who sinned, this man or his parents, that he was born blind?"

"Neither this man nor his parents sinned," said Jesus, "but this happened so that the works of God might be displayed in him. As long as it is day, we must do the works of him who sent me. Night is coming, when no one can work. While I am in the world, I am the light of the world."

After saying this, he spit on the ground, made some mud with the saliva, and put it on the man's eyes. "Go," he told

him, *"wash in the Pool of Siloam"* (this word means *"Sent"*).
So the man went and washed, and came home seeing.

*His neighbors and those who had formerly seen him begging
asked, "Isn't this the same man who used to sit and beg?"
Some claimed that he was.*

Others said, "No, he only looks like him."

But he himself insisted, "I am the man."

"How then were your eyes opened?" they asked.

*He replied, "The man they call Jesus made some mud and
put it on my eyes. He told me to go to Siloam and wash. So I
went and washed, and then I could see."*

John 9:1–11

14

Never Say Never

Nobody has ever heard of opening the eyes of a man born blind.

John 9:32

In the middle of the South Pacific, a tiny island called Pingelap dots the map. Its total landmass is less than three square miles, and the highest elevation on the island is ten feet above sea level. When Typhoon Lengkieki swept over the island in 1755, it destroyed all of its vegetation and drowned 90 percent of its inhabitants. The twenty survivors resorted to fishing as the only means of survival until the island revegetated.

After the great typhoon, a genetic peculiarity evolved. A surprisingly large proportion of the next generation was born color-blind. Everywhere else in the world, less than one in thirty thousand people is color-blind. On the island of Pingelap, one in twelve is born color-blind. The high percentage can be traced to the fact that several people in the surviving gene pool carried a rare genetic mutation responsible for congenital achromatopsia.

People with normal color vision have approximately seven million cones in their eyes that enable them to distinguish ten million different colors. Achromatopes have no functional cones. They rely exclusively on their low-light photoreceptor rods in the retina. As a result, they are so hypersensitive to light that they wear very dark wraparound sunglasses or avoid light altogether. Their poor vision forces them to use a monocle (the Monopoly man thing) to read text or see things from a distance.

The sad irony is that few places on earth are as beautiful or colorful as this tropical paradise. "It was striking how green everything was in Pingelap," notes Oliver Sacks in his book *The Island of the Colorblind*. "Not only the foliage of trees, but their fruits as well."[1] The brightly colored exotic fruits look as good as they taste, but the color-blind Pingelapians can't perceive them because of one genetic mutation.

Geneticists have discovered four causes of congenital achromatopsia. Three of them are mutations in the cone cell cyclic nucleotide-gated ion channels CNGA3 and CNGB3, as well as the cone cell transducin, GNAT2. The most recent discovery is a mutation of gene PDE6C, located on chromosome locus 10, 10q24.

When was the last time you thanked God for chromosome locus 10, 10q24? Or for any of those cells or chromosomes? Just sayin'.

The Mind's Eye

At about six months of age, children start developing internal pictures of the world around them. Psychologists call this ability to create and catalog mental images *representational intelligence*. Like a slow-developing Polaroid, those internal images are developed in your mind's eye.

The first internal image is usually mom, and it develops at around six months of age. Dad doesn't enter the picture until eight months. Give children a few years, and their entire vocabulary will have a matching picture. But if your eyesight doesn't develop normally, neither will your representational intelligence.

Think of it this way: words prompt images.

If I say *the White House*, a picture of 1600 Pennsylvania Avenue pops into your mind. And the same is true of *lake* or *car* or *pet*. A representation of each pops up, though we all fill in the blanks differently. I see Lake Ida in Alexandria, Minnesota; my first car, a 1985 Dodge Colt we called the Batmobile; and our dog, Michaelangelo.

What's that have to do with the sixth sign?

The man born blind had more than enough words in his vocabulary, but his photo album was empty. He couldn't picture the faces of his mother or father. He'd heard his friends describe that magnificent Jerusalem sunset, but he couldn't imagine it because he'd never seen one. The guy couldn't even pick himself out of a lineup.

Imagine closing your eyes and never being able to open them again. That would still be better than where this guy was at, because you could at least see pictures in your memory. But he had never seen *anything*. This was the only world the man born blind had ever known.

This moment is hard to fully grasp because we just can't unsee what we've seen. It's impossible to imagine, but I think we'll experience something similar when we cross the space-time continuum. We'll finally hear angelic sounds that physical ears just couldn't handle. We'll see celestial colors that were invisible to our eyes.

What'll we see first?

I think this miracle is a good clue: we'll see exactly what the man born blind saw first—Jesus' face!

Good Eye

During my (Mark's) senior year of high school, my basketball coach noticed I was squinting while at the free throw line, so he suggested I get my vision checked out. I thought my vision was fine, but the ophthalmologist informed me that I had 20/40 vision. I was seeing at twenty feet what people with normal vision could see at forty feet, which might explain my terrible free throw percentage!

You can keep it together with 20/40 vision—you can get a driver's license, read print, and recognize faces, more or less. It's just that distant objects look blurry.

I'll never forget the car ride home after putting in contacts for the first time. I almost can't put it into words. It was only about a five-minute drive, and we'd made that drive a thousand times. But it was like I was seeing the world for the very first time! I remember seeing some pink and purple flowers that were so vivid and so colorful and so beautiful I could hardly believe my eyes.

I was finally able to see what had always been there!

The man born blind had to be freaking out about every single image, but he saw them for what they are—miracles.

> Your eye is the lamp of your body. When your eye is healthy, your whole body is full of light, but when it is bad, your body is full of darkness.[2]

We don't see the world as it is. We see the world as we are.

I can't read this verse without hearing my Little League baseball coach yelling, "Good eye, good eye!" I guess he meant I was doing a good job at not swinging at bad pitches. In the biblical context, it means looking at things from a God's-eye view. And when you look at life through your good eye, you discover that there is more to *everything* than meets the eye!

The only difference between seeing the miracles and missing them is which eye you're looking through. Jewish rabbis made a distinction between a *good eye* and *bad eye*. Both had to do with a person's attitude toward others. A bad eye turned a blind eye to the poor. A good eye is your ability to spot opportunities to bless others.

Every *Ology*

I (Mark) split my undergrad education between polar opposites— the University of Chicago and Central Bible College. The curriculum at Central laid a theological foundation for everything from pneumatology to soteriology to eschatology.[3] But if you asked me which undergraduate class had the greatest influence on my theology (and if you don't care, I'll tell you anyway), I would have to say it was a class on immunology at the University of Chicago Hospital Center. The professor didn't refer to God once in her lectures. I'm not so sure she believed in God. But every lecture on the immune system was a brilliant exegesis of Psalm 139:14: "I praise you because I am fearfully and wonderfully made." I'm pretty sure I walked out of one of those classes praising God for hemoglobin.

That class gave me such a profound appreciation for the intricacies of the immune system. In a lot of ways, this led me to believe that *every ology is a branch of theology.*

God has revealed different facets of who He is in a lot of ways. The most obvious is Scripture. But the sneakiest is nature. And if you turn a blind eye to natural revelation, special revelation isn't as special. Albert Einstein said it best: "Science without religion is lame, and religion without science is blind."[4]

Whether they know it or not, the astronomer who charts stars, the geneticist who maps genomes, the oceanographer who explores the deep sea craters, the ornithologist who studies and preserves rare bird species, and the physicist who tries to catch quarks are all studying the Creator—by studying His creation.

There will always be scientists who reject intelligent design. But just because they keep faith out of science doesn't mean we should keep science out of faith. In my experience, science adds legitimacy to theology. My library is filled with books about entomology and neurology and ophthalmology. I know just enough about those subjects to be dangerous, but all of it has increased my appreciation for the Creator and His creation.

Some miracles just don't make sense without science. And the sixth miracle is one of them. Just as a little chemistry enhances our appreciation of Jesus mutating water molecules, a little neurology goes a long way toward explaining the miraculous healing of a man born blind.

Synaptogenesis

We generally take sight for granted unless we lose it, but even the simplest process is divinely complex. The retina sitting at the back of your eye (the thing that gives you evil red eyes in pictures) conducts close to ten billion calculations every second, and that's before an image even travels through the optic nerve to the visual cortex. Dr. John Stevens puts it this way:

> To simulate 10 milliseconds of the complete processing of even a single nerve cell from the retina would require about 500 simultaneous non-linear differential equations one hundred times and would take at least several minutes of processing on a Cray supercomputer. Keeping in mind that there are more than 10 million cells interacting with each other in complex ways, it would take a minimum of a hundred years of Cray time to simulate what takes place in your eye every second.[5]

Honestly, I have no idea what that even means. But that's kind of the point.

Ears that hear and eyes that see—the LORD has made them both.[6]

I'll be the first to say I totally flip through verses like this. No double take. It would take a lifetime of research to understand all the optical and auditory nuances of just this one verse of Scripture. But the sixth miracle goes way beyond just healing blind eyes.

Four primary types of healing miracles are repeated in the Gospels. Jesus made the lame walk, the mute talk, the blind see, and the deaf hear. You know this. They're all amazing, and blindness is the most difficult because of how complex the human eye is. But the sixth miracle is in a category all by itself. Jesus doesn't just heal a guy who got blind somewhere along the way; He heals a man *born* blind. The significance of that is this: there were *no* synaptic connections between the optic nerve and visual cortex in this blind man's brain. Simply put: if the nerves from the eye to the brain are a road, this road isn't a damaged or sketchy road—there's just straight up no road.

This healing miracle wasn't simple. Jesus creates a synaptic pathway that didn't exist.

This is nothing short of *synaptogenesis*. Look it up.

On day forty-two after conception, the first neuron is formed in a baby's brain. By birth a baby will have an estimated eighty-six billion brain cells.[7] As a newborn experiences new sights and sounds, the brain begins to form connections in its little baby brain called synapses. Almost like telephone wires that crisscross a city, synapses crisscross the cerebral cortex. By the time a baby is six months old, each brain cell has about eighteen thousand connections. Maybe more if you listened to Baby Mozart. But if not, that's cool too!

This miraculous process is called synaptogenesis. If the human mind is God's masterpiece, then synaptogenesis is Symphony No. 5 in C Minor.

Dr. Harry Chugani (a smart guy who invented PET scans) compares the process to a nuclear reactor. Millions of neurons are firing across billions of neural pathways every second of every day. According to Dr. Chugani, a baby's brain pulsates at about 225 times the rate of the average adult. Babysitters, you know what I'm talking about. No wonder it's so hard to keep kids in a high chair.

Never Say Never

Babies are born legally blind.

At birth, their vision is no better than 20/200, and they can't focus on anything farther than twelve inches away. That's why touch is so critical in the early stages of a baby's life. That's how they interpret the world: by feeling it out. But after eight months, their color vision and depth perception kick in.

Vision pretty much develops somewhere between birth and eighteen months, and synaptogenesis in the visual cortex peaks at about three months. That's where this miracle gets fascinating. If you were to place a patch over the eye of a newborn baby and leave it there during the first few years of life, that baby would be blind in that eye for the rest of their life, even if there was nothing wrong with the eye. The reason is simple: no synapses would form between the visual cortex and optical nerve.

Now, back to the man born blind.

Ophthalmologists would pretty much call this guy blind for good. No fixing that problem. The natural window of opportunity had closed. But God just so happens to do some of His finest work when we're done for. The childbearing years passed Sarah *waaaaay* before Isaac was born, but that didn't keep God from getting the job done. And God conceived a child in a virgin. Amazing.

Do you ever feel like you've missed your window of opportunity?

Those are the people Jesus healed—the woman with the issue of blood, the woman at the well, the tax collector, the leper, and the woman caught in the act of adultery. The full spectrum gets some love from Jesus. I think He was being pretty obvious about who He can heal: everyone.

I don't know your specific circumstances, but I do know that God can create a new synaptic pathway or repair an old one. He's the God of second chances, and third and fourth and thousandth.

When Jesus gets involved, *never say never*!

15

The Miracle League

Who sinned, this man or his parents, that he was born blind?

John 9:2

My friends John and Tricia Tiller went through pretty much every parent's worst nightmare. Their three-year-old son accidentally fell out of a second-story playroom window. Eli was medivaced to the hospital where he was comatose for three weeks. He miraculously survived, but not without significant brain damage. Eli had to relearn every basic motor function from speech to walking. And despite the prayers of his parents and endless hours of physical therapy, Eli still has significant limitations. He has limited peripheral vision out of both eyes, and the left side of his body still has limited motor skills. So Eli speaks with a severe stutter and walks with a pronounced limp, but he can sing pretty doggone good. His pitch isn't perfect, but there wasn't a dry eye when he sang for National Community Church.

John and Tricia have thanked God countless times for saving their son, but their prayers for miraculous healing have gone unanswered. They've done everything humanly possible to help their son and spent tens of thousands of dollars on uninsured medical equipment. For the first three years postsurgery, they spent 80 percent of every waking hour in therapy. And they continued to believe that God was going to heal their son. In John's words, "We waited and waited. We knew that one day we'd be standing in front of crowds saying, 'Look what the Lord has done! He has completely healed our son.' But that's not what happened."

What about the miracle you're believing God for that just isn't happening? What happens when nothing goes down?

Sometimes you need to keep holding out, like the woman with the issue of blood who held out and held on for twelve long years.[1] But sometimes you need to accept the new normal and recognize that God might want to glorify Himself in a way you wouldn't choose. And it takes tremendous spiritual discernment to know when to believe what. In John's words:

> After three years of doing everything we could for our son, it was time to accept his current condition and choose to live life with disability. This disability was something we couldn't remove, and evidently God was choosing to not completely heal Eli. So we had to burn our old scripts and look for what God could do with our new script. So for the past five years, we've accepted life with disability. That doesn't mean I've stopped praying for my son. Like any father, I'd give my right arm to see my son healed. But instead of getting discouraged or getting angry, I choose to look for what God can do.[2]

Why, God?

When the dust settled for the Tillers, John began to interrogate God with the usual *why* questions:

"Why, God? Why do little boys fall from windows? Why did my little boy fall from that window? Why him? Why me?" I looked to Scripture for an answer, and it turns out that "Why, God?" isn't a new question at all.[3]

John, appropriately, found his answer in John's Gospel. The family and friends of the man born blind made a false assumption. They assumed his parents had sinned and their son was being punished for it. It was hard enough being blind, but to carry the weight of responsibility for something that wasn't even his fault must have been unbearable. I mean, what the heck? They weren't exactly discreet when they asked Jesus, "Who sinned, this man or his parents?"[4] They assumed it was a a sin issue, or a lack of faith. But it was none of the above. Then Jesus set the record straight by revealing the real reason:

This happened so that the works of God might be displayed in him.[5]

When life or biology doesn't go according to plan, we naturally look for someone or something to blame. That tendency goes all the way back to the Garden of Eden when Eve whips out the first excuse: "The devil made me do it." But no one wins the blame game! And it's usually followed by a postgame pity party.

At some point, you have to realize that the circumstances we ask God to change are usually the circumstances that God's using to change us. We don't always get an answer to our *why* questions (for now), but sometimes God does leave clues.

Of course John wanted to play catch with his son in the yard. But Eli can't do that. However, he was drafted by the Miracle League—a baseball league for kids with special needs. At first, John was afraid that he was setting up his son to fail. But there's only one rule in the Miracle League—every kid gets a hit, every kid gets on base, and every kid scores! They play on a rubberized field for wheelchair accessibility, and each kid has a teenage or adult buddy.

"If you saw them play," John says, "you'd call it a miracle."

Sometimes the miracle we want isn't the one we get. God gives us a different one.

About a year ago, the Miracle League did a black-tie fundraiser hosted by the local minor league baseball team. A few major leaguers, including Javier Lopez, showed up. But it was Eli who stole the show by leading the crowd in a rousing rendition of "Take Me Out to the Ball Game." No dry eyes there either! Eli has that effect. By the end of the night, he helped them raise a ton of money so kids like him could play ball too. He even signed a few autographs!

There are still a lot of chapters left in Eli's life, but John can see the story line God's got for his son. He says, "We've seen lots of miracles that I don't have time to share. But there is one thing I can tell you for sure: those miracles never would have happened if life had gone according to my old script."

Anti-Miracles

Have you ever prayed for something and literally gotten the exact opposite? The girl you asked to prom actually throws chicken at you and goes with your best friend? I call it an anti-answer to prayer. It's happened to me more than once! In fact, it happened twice with the same prayer.

During the early days of National Community Church, the church office was a spare bedroom in our (Mark's) house. Then when our daughter, Summer, was born, it became her bedroom by night and the church office by day. The commute was amazing, but it got old real fast. NCC was meeting in the movie theaters at Union Station, so we decided to look for a row house in that neighborhood that we could convert into a church office.

We found the perfect place. Twice. The layout and location were beyond ideal, and so was the price. Obviously we prayed like crazy, but both of them were sold out from under us the night before the day we presented our offer! Double sucker punch. I literally just stopped looking. My faith was deflated. Then one day a few weeks later, I was walking by 205 F Street NE—a row house one block from Union Station. The only downside was that it was right next to a crack house, but that downside was its upside. We had no idea at the time we purchased 205 F Street NE that the crack house next door would become Ebenezer's coffeehouse. But God knew. And that's why He closed the door on those other two properties.

Here's a lesson I've learned: you really can't claim half a promise. We love asking God to open doors, a la Revelation 3:8–9. But part of being okay with Him opening doors is being okay with Him closing doors as well. Those closed doors would act a little more like trapdoors if we actually walked through them. When God closes a door, it often seems like an anti-miracle. But what seems like a setback is God setting you up for something bigger and better. If we hadn't purchased 205 F Street NE, we never would've been able to pull off our coffeehouse construction project. What seemed like a double fail turned into a double miracle—205 *and* 201 F Street NE.

The Glory of God

A few months ago a friend of mine was diagnosed with cancer, and we've been praying for spontaneous remission (that's the medical term for miracle). Unfortunately, tests were rolling in the wrong direction at his first follow-up visit. When he called me, it was tough to know what to say. What *does* one say in that scenario, you know? The truth is, there's not much to say, and it's really better to listen than to talk. But then I felt like I needed to remind him of a simple yet difficult truth: "I'm going to keep praying for your healing, but healing isn't the ultimate goal. The ultimate goal is God's glory."

I'd love for God to glorify Himself by healing my friend, but even if my friend is healed, that isn't the ultimate goal. The goal isn't the miracle. The goal is God's glory. And if you forget that, it's difficult to get through difficult circumstances. Miracles are just happy side effects. So I'll say this: the will of God is the glory of God. That's why cancer can't keep you from doing the will of God. Nothing can. You can glorify God under any and every circumstance.

No good parent wishes pain or suffering on their kid, but at the same time, you can't just pray away every problem. Obviously, parents still pray a hedge of protection around their kids. But it's stupid to think that the will of God is an insurance plan. It's a dangerous plan. Just read Hebrews 11:

> I do not have time to tell about Gideon, Barak, Samson and Jephthah, about David and Samuel and the prophets, who through faith conquered kingdoms, administered justice, and gained what was promised; who shut the mouths of lions, quenched the fury of the flames, and escaped the edge of the sword; whose weakness was turned to strength; and who became powerful in battle and routed foreign armies. Women received back their dead, raised to life again.[6]

If only the chapter ended there. It doesn't.

> There were others who were tortured, refusing to be released so that they might gain an even better resurrection. Some faced jeers and flogging, and even chains and imprisonment. They were put to death by stoning; they were sawed in two; they were killed by the sword. They went about in sheepskins and goatskins, destitute, persecuted and mistreated—the world was not worthy of them.[7]

Were only half of them in the will of God? The ones who conquered kingdoms or shut the mouths of lions? Or were all of them in the will of God—including the ones who were sawed in two?

The will of God isn't safe. It might just get you killed. But if God gets the glory, then the goal is accomplished. And the eternal reward we receive will be well worth any sacrifices.

The will of God isn't linear. It's not algebra. It doesn't add up. Eternity belongs in the equation. And if my friend isn't healed until he reaches the other side of the space-time continuum, it'll be no less miraculous.

You'll Get Through This

Right before he released his thirtieth book, *You'll Get through This*, we had the privilege of hosting Max Lucado at National Community Church. Max shared a story about his friend JJ Jasper, whose five-year-old son, Cooper, was killed in a dune buggy crash.[8] What started out as a carefree father-son outing turned into tragedy when the buggy flipped over, and Cooper died just hours later. And JJ's grief was coupled with guilt because he was the driver.

After calling 911, JJ then had to call his wife and share the news. Before making the call, the Holy Spirit gave him the words to say, just as He promised He would do during life's most difficult moments. JJ said, "I've got some bad news to share, but before I tell you, I want you to think about everything that you know that is good about God."

Max decided to do what JJ prescribed. He knew he might need that checklist someday too. So Max went on a little hunt through the Bible for the goodness of God. Here's a short list he came up with, and it's helped him get through many of the trials he's faced:

God is still sovereign no matter what. He still knows my name. Angels still respond to his call. The hearts of rulers still bend at his bidding. The death of Jesus still saves souls. The Spirit of God still dwells in saints. Heaven is still only heartbeats away. The grave is still temporary housing. God is still faithful. He's not caught off guard. He uses everything for his glory and my ultimate good. He uses tragedy to accomplish his will and his will is right, holy, and perfect. Sorrow may come with the night, but joy comes with the morning.[9]

The Bible doesn't talk about our blind friend's parents much, but they were probably pretty bummed. Call it emotional whiplash. There aren't answers for that type of thing, so sometimes you have to just lean on God (by sometimes, of course, I mean all the time).

That's exactly what JJ did. And that's what got him through the most difficult chapter in his life. In JJ's words, "People with good intentions say time heals wounds. That's not true. You'll never get over it. When you lose a loved one you care deeply about, you'll never get over it, but you will get through it."[10]

Why do children fall out of windows?

Why do kids die in dune buggy accidents?

Why are babies born blind?

Those are questions you take to the grave. But you can't let the questions you can't answer keep you from trusting what you know to be true.

God's good, all the time. All the time, God's good.

In the words of Corrie ten Boom, "There is no pit too deep that God's grace isn't deeper still."[11]

Explanatory Style

In his book *Learned Optimism*, Dr. Martin Seligman explains that we all have an "explanatory style" to explain life's experiences. In his words, "Explanatory style is the manner in which you habitually explain to yourself why events happen."[12]

Let's say you're at a restaurant waiting for a date you were supposed to meet at 7:00 sharp, but forty-five minutes later he or she is a no-show. At some point you need to explain to yourself why the person isn't there. You might think, "He stood me up," and then get mad. You could jump to conclusions and think, "She doesn't love me anymore," and *boom*, you're sad. You could assume, "He was in an accident," making you anxious. You might imagine, "He's working overtime so that he can pay for our meal," causing you to feel grateful. You could think, "She's with another man," bringing some jealousy into the mix. Heck, you might realize, "This gives me a perfect excuse to break up with her," giving you a great deal of relief.

Same situation.

Very different explanations.

There are lots of different explanations for every experience. Options. And while you can't control your experiences, you *can* control your explanations. Biblically speaking, your explanations are actually more important than your experiences. When bad things happen to us, it's easy to play the victim card. But you're not a victim.

If anybody had the right to play victim, it was Joseph. Everything that could go wrong, did go wrong with this poor guy. He got backhanded by his brothers, sold into slavery, and accused of a crime he straight up didn't commit. But after seventeen years of things going from bad to worse, he reveals the explanatory style that got him through the tough times:

> You intended to harm me, but God intended it for good to accomplish what is now being done, the saving of many lives.[13]

Bitter or better? Depends on your explanatory style, I guess.

In the words of Aldous Huxley, "Experience is not what happens to you; it is what you do with what happens to you."[14]

A few years ago a college cheerleader hobbled into church on crutches. When I asked her what happened, she could barely hold back the tears. She had torn her Achilles tendon, had to have surgery to repair it, and was in a cast for eight weeks. Four days after getting her cast off, she re-tore the same tendon stepping on a patch of ice and had to have a second surgery. But, in typical fashion, God redeemed her rehab to resurrect her dream of becoming an athletic trainer. She got some killer hands-on experience. It was a tough test, but she aced the exam with her explanatory style.

I don't know why bad things happen to good people or why good things happen to bad people. But I do know this: "in all things God works for the good of those who love him, who have been called according to his purpose."[15] If you allow Him, He'll recycle your pain for someone else's gain. And if you're really lucky, it can work for your gain as well. The man born blind didn't get the first half of his life back, but I bet he enjoyed that second half twice as much.

Go and Wash

Like a bunch of Jesus' miracles, this one comes with an instruction manual. He tells the man to go and wash in the Pool of Siloam.[16] We don't really know the exact distance he traveled to get to the pool, but it was definitely a hike. I've actually hiked through Hezekiah's tunnel, which connects the Gihon Spring with the Pool of Siloam. The man born blind would have descended hundreds of steps, and this miracle happened during the Feast of Tabernacles, so he would have bumped into tens of thousands of pilgrims.

Why would Jesus send this blind man on a scavenger hunt? This seems like a mean joke. Why not just heal him on the spot?

Hold that thought.

I recently heard a story told by an Episcopal bishop named William Frey.[17] As a young man, he volunteered to tutor a student who was blind. The student had lost his sight at the age of thirteen in a chemical explosion. It's easy to feel like life is over at that point. The only thing greater than his self-pity was his hatred toward God. For six months after the accident, all he did was feel sorry for himself. Then one day his father said, "John, winter's coming and the storm windows need to be up—that's your job. I want those hung by the time I get back this evening or else!" Then he pretended to walk out of the room, slamming the door. John got *mad*! He was so angry that he decided to just do it. He thought, *When I fall, they'll have a blind and paralyzed son*! But John didn't fall. He discovered he was capable of doing far more than he realized, even with blind eyes. He also later learned that his dad was never more than five feet away. He shadowed his son to make sure he was safe, but he knew that helplessness is a far worse curse than blindness.

I'm not entirely sure why Jesus had this blind man go on a mission just to take a bath, but I'm guessing that he'd lived a relatively helpless life. He depended on everybody for everything. So Jesus didn't just heal his blind eyes. He restored his dignity by expelling helplessness.

Scripture's pretty clear when it comes to the sequence of this miracle. It says he "came back seeing."[18] If he hadn't taken this step of faith and gone to the Pool of Siloam, I don't think he would've come back seeing! And that's one secret to experiencing the miraculous: *most miracles require an act of blind obedience.*

You can't manufacture miracles, but you can wash in the Pool of Siloam.

One step of obedience can open your eyes.

THE SEVENTH SIGN

When Mary reached the place where Jesus was and saw him, she fell at his feet and said, "Lord, if you had been here, my brother would not have died."

When Jesus saw her weeping, and the Jews who had come along with her also weeping, he was deeply moved in spirit and troubled. "Where have you laid him?" he asked.

"Come and see, Lord," they replied.

Jesus wept.

Then the Jews said, "See how he loved him!"

But some of them said, "Could not he who opened the eyes of the blind man have kept this man from dying?"

Jesus, once more deeply moved, came to the tomb. It was a cave with a stone laid across the entrance. "Take away the stone," he said.

"But, Lord," said Martha, the sister of the dead man, "by this time there is a bad odor, for he has been there four days."

Then Jesus said, "Did I not tell you that if you believe, you will see the glory of God?"

So they took away the stone. Then Jesus looked up and said, "Father, I thank you that you have heard me. I knew that you always hear me, but I said this for the benefit of the people standing here, that they may believe that you sent me."

When he had said this, Jesus called in a loud voice, "Lazarus, come out!" The dead man came out, his hands and feet wrapped with strips of linen, and a cloth around his face.

Jesus said to them, "Take off the grave clothes and let him go."

John 11:32–44

16

The Grave Robber

If you had been here, my brother would not have died. But I know that even now God will give you whatever you ask.

John 11:21–22

One of my (Mark's) earliest movie memories is the 1978 version of *Superman* starring Christopher Reeve. You probably weren't alive, but I'll fill you in. Superman's crush, Lois Lane, is driving through the Nevada desert when a crevice opened by an earthquake swallows her car. Superman can't get there in time to save Lois because he's building a natural dam out of boulders to stop a flood caused by a breach in the Hoover Dam. When he discovers that Lois is dead, Superman gets super angry. He flies around the earth at supersonic speed, reversing its rotation, theoretically turning back time.

I know the science behind that scene is suspect. Hey, it was 1978. We know the earth rotates around its axis at one thousand miles per hour. If Superman had reversed its rotation, he may have saved Lois Lane, but everyone else on the planet would have died of whiplash! Don't you wish you could turn back time right after saying or doing something you wish you hadn't? Sadly, the arrow of time points in one direction.

What's done is done. Some things in life are irreversible.

You can't unbake cookies, uncut hair, or unrun red lights. I've learned those lessons the hard way. Some of those lessons were easily laughed off after a little embarrassment—like the bald strip on the back of my head after the barber said, "Oops." I literally used Lora's mascara for a few weeks until the bald spot grew back out. Others cost a little more, like a $110 ticket for running a red light. But there are those irreversible moments that leave a hole in your heart forever—like standing at the foot of my father-in-law's casket after a heart attack ended his young earthly life.

One of those painful lessons came during my sophomore basketball season in college. Not only did we lose our last game and bow out of the national tournament, but I also tore my anterior cruciate ligament in the fourth quarter. When the doctor gave me his diagnosis, I asked him when it would be a-okay. He said *never*. Turns out, I needed to have reconstructive surgery because torn ligaments don't actually heal. At that point in my life basketball *was* my life. Life as I knew it was pretty much over.

You probably know the feeling all too well: your worst fears, the irreversible ones, just became reality. Welcome to Mary and Martha's world. Their brother was gone for good. Then again, it's not over until God says it's over.

Enter Jesus.

He was four days late, but he was about to do something absolutely unprecedented. He'd reversed withered arms and weather systems. But the seventh miracle was a sudden-death showdown with an undefeated opponent. The Grave Robber had it out with death itself, and death met its match.

The Law of Entropy

The second law of thermodynamics states that if left to its own devices, everything in the universe moves toward disorder and decay. In English: cars rust, food rots, and, of course, humans grow old and die. It takes many forms, but it's called the law of entropy. The only way to prevent entropy is to introduce an outside energy source to counteract it. The technical term is negentropy, and the refrigerator is a perfect example. If you plug it into an electrical outlet, it produces cold air that keeps food from rotting. If, however, the refrigerator gets unplugged from its power source, entropy takes over again. Trust me—once our family returned from a Christmas vacation and I knew something was off before we even walked in the front door. The smell was that bad.

Speaking of stink, I'm sure Mary and Martha had to hold their breath when Jesus told the mourners to roll away the stone. They were afraid it would stink to high heaven, but Jesus was about to counteract four days of decomposition with one miracle of negentropy.

The law of entropy doesn't just govern the physical universe. It has governed the spiritual realm since it was introduced in the Garden of Eden after Adam and Eve's original sin. They had been forewarned: "You must not eat from the tree of the knowledge of good and evil, for when you eat from it you will certainly die."[1] They didn't die immediately after eating the forbidden fruit, but their disobedience introduced the process of decay that leads to physical and spiritual death. Sin is a slow-acting poison. Its immediate effects are sneaky, but the aftereffects are way nastier than what we realize at the time. Original sin caused a disturbance in the Force, so to speak (going back to '70s movies and *Star Wars*). It introduced sickness and suffering to the equation of life. Everything from genetic defects to natural disasters trace their origins back to original sin. We live in a fallen world—everything is affected by entropy.

Just like Adam and Eve discovered, sin opens the door to entropy. The more you sin, the quicker you begin to decay. Sin's a matter of life and death. Jesus didn't die just to make bad people good. He brings dead people to life! And Lazarus is exhibit A.

Do the Lazarus

The seventh miracle is way better if you know a little about Jewish burial traditions. I'll fill you in. When Lazarus died, his feet would have been bound at the ankles and his arms would have been tied to his body with linen strips. Then his corpse would have been wrapped in approximately one hundred pounds of graveclothes to protect and preserve the body. Some scholars believe that the head itself would have been wrapped with so many linens that it would measure a foot wide. So the best mental image is probably the one that immediately comes to mind—Lazarus looked like a mummy.

It seems to me like two miracles happen here, not one. The first one is resurrection. But how in the world did Lazarus get up and get out of the tomb in a full-body cast? That's the second miracle! I'm not sure I can re-create the scene, but Lazarus didn't walk out of the tomb. I think he had no choice but to hop out.

> The dead man came out, his hands and feet wrapped with strips of linen, and a cloth around his face.[2]

Maybe my imagination gets a little carried away, but I bet his friends and family "did the Lazarus" at dance parties every chance they got. Lazarus *had* to bust a move to get out of that tomb. And once again, Jesus turns tragedy into comedy. When Lazarus comes hopping out of the tomb, they were able to laugh about it the rest of their lives.

Now let me get serious. If you miss this, you miss the point. This miracle doesn't just foreshadow Jesus' own resurrection. It foreshadows yours. It's not just something Jesus did for Lazarus.

It's a snapshot of what Jesus wants to do in your life every day. When we sin, it's like the enemy throws some more graveclothes on us. Sin can bury you alive and turn you into a mummy. But Jesus is hollering into the tomb.

I like to replace people's names in Scripture with mine sometimes. Helps me personalize it. So take out Lazarus's name and insert your own: *Mark, come out!*

Can you hear Him call your name?

Hop out of your tomb.

Second Life

Church tradition offers two versions of what happened to Lazarus after his resurrection. Some say he and his sisters made their way to the island of Cyprus, where Lazarus became first bishop of Kition. The Church of Saint Lazarus, in the modern city of Larnaca, is believed by some to be built over his second tomb, which he was buried in some thirty years after his first death. A second church tradition holds that Lazarus and his sisters ended up in Marseille, France, where Lazarus survived the persecution of Christians by Nero by hiding in a tomb, appropriately enough, but eventually died by beheading during the persecution ordered by Emperor Domitian.[3]

I'm not sure which tradition is true (if either of them is). But either way, Jesus gave Mary and Martha their brother back, and Lazarus lived two lives. How long he lived after he died, we don't know for sure. But Jesus literally gave him a second life. And the Grave Robber wants to do for you what He did for Lazarus. But He doesn't just want to give back the life that sin and Satan have stolen. He came that you might have life and have it more abundantly![4] The Son of God entered space-time so that you could exit it—so that you could spend eternity with Him in a place where entropy isn't a thing. Heaven is the end of entropy as we

145

know it, and death is defeated once and for all. In the words of the apostle Paul:

> Where, O death, is your victory?
> Where, O death, is your sting?[5]

When my (Mark's) father-in-law died, Parker and Summer were so young that they can't now remember him. So we would often tell stories when they were younger to help create some memories. During one of those conversations, Parker said, "I wish I could have said good-bye to Grandpa and told him to say hi to Jesus." In an overly excited voice, Summer responded, "When we die, we'll get to go to heaven and see Grandpa Schmidgall." To which Parker replied, "You shouldn't get so excited about dying!"

Remember when Jesus said we must become like little children? I think this is one dimension of that. At some point, the fear of death messes with the anticipation of eternal life. But there's no sense in fearing something that happens one way or another. After all, the purpose of life isn't to arrive safely at death.

There's nothing wrong with wanting to live a long life, but death shouldn't be something we dread. Death was defeated two thousand years ago. And to be absent from the body is to be present with the Lord.[6] So death is something we can actually anticipate because it's not the end! It's a new beginning. And many of the miracles we hoped for on earth will finally be fulfilled in heaven. Death is sort of a toll you have to pay, but it's worth it to get in!

Even Now

Lazarus has died, and for your sake I am glad that I was not there.

John 11:14–15 ESV

Let this be a lesson to all of you. It's one thing to forget a wedding you're supposed to attend. It's another thing to forget a wedding you're supposed to officiate. I mean, wow. Maybe it's because we didn't do a rehearsal the night before, but it totally slipped my (Mark's) mind.

Have you ever had a phone call trigger your memory? You see your boss's name pop up and you know *exactly* why they're calling. The moment my phone rang, my stomach was in my throat because I remembered the noon wedding I was supposed to officiate. It was one o'clock and I was in a dressing room at the mall. I died a thousand deaths in that dressing room. The bride and groom started worrying about their no-show pastor around quarter to noon, but it took more than an hour to track down my cell phone number. And how they got it is nothing short of miraculous. They called the church office, but we're closed on Saturdays. Somehow the call got transferred to the emergency phone in the elevator at Ebenezer's coffeehouse. Our pastor of discipleship, Heather Zempel, happened to be on the elevator when the call came in. She actually thought it was a prank call because she couldn't imagine me forgetting a wedding, but I was guilty as charged.

I showered, threw on a suit, and drove to the wedding venue like it was the NASCAR Sprint Cup Series. I arrived at 3:00 sharp, and the ceremony commenced. It wasn't easy making eye contact with the wedding guests, but the bride and groom were unbelievably gracious. They still attend our church. So don't tell me miracles don't happen!

When I finally got there, I decided not to say what Jesus said when He was late to Lazarus's funeral. I *didn't* say, "For your sake I am glad I was not there."[1]

Why on earth would Jesus say that?

Sounds mean, doesn't it? If your friend is on his deathbed and you have the ability to heal him, don't you drop everything and get there as quickly as possible? But, no. Jesus stays put for two days. Then He takes His sweet time getting there. *Why?*

Passive-Aggressive

When Jesus finally shows up four days late, Mary and Martha get a little passive-aggressive with Him. They both say the exact same thing: "If you had been here, my brother would not have died."[2] They aren't really blaming Jesus . . . but they are, but they aren't, but they are. I know I can be passive-aggressive with God. I don't necessarily blame Him for the bad things that happen, but He could have kept them from happening. So why doesn't He?

Why wouldn't Jesus just teleport to Bethany and heal Lazarus?

Here's what I think. Jesus had been there and done that. It would be too predictable for Jesus to walk across water, arrive in the nick of time, and heal Laz as he was drawing his last breath. Jesus had already revealed His healing power. It was time to whip out His *resurrection power.*

This is simple logic: you can't ressurect something that's not dead. If you feel like you're stuck in a rut, God may be getting ready to do something more miraculous than you've previously experienced. But something precious might have to die first so He can resurrect it.

If Jesus had simply healed Lazarus, I'm sure some there would be praising God. I'm also sure some skeptics would have claimed he wasn't actually *that* sick. But when someone's been dead for four days, there's pretty much only one explanation.

Healing Laz before he died would have definitely reinforced the faith they already had. But Jesus wanted to *stretch* their faith. It's just a fact of life: sometimes things have to go from bad to worse before they get better!

God's Grammar

I forget most sermons I hear, and I'm sure our congregation has forgotten most of mine. You probably don't remember the first half of this book. That's fine. But every once in a while, there's a moment of revelation in the middle of a message that has that special something-something. It's life altering. That's what I experienced listening to an old sermon by Dr. Charles Crabtree titled "God's Grammar." One little line is absolutely unforgettable: "Never put a comma where God puts a period and never put a period where God puts a comma."

When someone dies, that is nature's period. Game over. But Jesus knew He would take it into overtime with a Hail Mary, so to speak. When He heard the news that Laz was sick, Jesus made a bold prediction: "This sickness will not end in death."[3] I used to have a problem with that statement because it seems like Jesus is wrong, right? After all, Lazarus dies. But the operative word is *end*. Jesus said the sickness would not *end* in death, and it didn't. He knew Lazarus would die, but Jesus didn't put a period there. He just inserted a four-day comma.

"Sometimes it looks like God is missing the mark," observed Oswald Chambers, "because we're too short-sighted to see what He's aiming for."[4]

Have you ever felt like God was a day late or a dollar short?

Well, it looks like He's four days late here. But if you've learned anything so far, it should be that it's not over until God says it's over. He gets the final word. And Martha knew it. This has to be one of the greatest statements of faith in all of Scripture:

> Lord . . . if you had been here, my brother would not have died. But I know that even now God will give you whatever you ask.[5]

Did you catch the conjunction? There's an important *but* sandwiched between the fact and faith.

Evidently, Martha's still holding out hope four days after the funeral. To be honest, this looks more like a psychotic break than faith, you know? Like she's in denial. At what point do you stop hoping and get to grieving? Day one? Day two? Day four? But this is how faith works: it looks like it's out of touch with reality, but that's because it's in touch with a reality that's more real than anything you can see or hear or taste or touch or smell with your five senses. Sometimes if you're in touch with God, it looks an awful lot like you're out of touch with reality.

The sentence should end after Martha says, "If you had been here, my brother would not have died." But there's no period. Faith inserts a comma, even at the end of a death sentence: "Even now God will give you whatever you ask."

Risk Your Reputation

When he was twenty-five years old, Clayton King led a fifty-mile backpacking trip into the Himalaya mountains to share the gospel with some folks in the Zanskar Valley.[6] I should note: they don't get out much. Along with the physical challenge of making the mountainous hike, there's also the risk of being kidnapped or killed. A few months before their trip, a group of European missionaries was executed by Islamic militants for attempting to smuggle eleven Bibles across the border. Clayton and his friends had *eleven hundred* Bibles in their backpacks!

In preparation for their missionary journey, the team did water-only fasts, trained with weighted backpacks, and read as much as they could about Tibetan Buddhism. One of the team members was a doctor, so they manufactured a mobile medical clinic to take with them. And they prayed for miracles, because they knew they'd need them. Lots of them, on the regular.

The five-person team flew into Leh, one of the highest airports in the world. After acclimating to the 11,000-foot elevation, they traveled along the Kashmiri border with Pakistan toward a remote village called Zangla. On the way there, one divine appointment set the tone for the rest of the trip. In the middle of nowhere, they came across a hitchhiker who was standing by the side of the road. For all they knew, this man could be a terrorist, so the team protested when their native-born driver pulled over to pick him up. Clayton objected so vehemently that the hitchhiker said in his broken English, "You are a very loud-talking boy." Then he revealed why the driver stopped: "My name is Raja Norbu, and I am the king of the Zanskar Valley. I live in a small village called Zangla. It is very far from here and difficult to reach. As provincial governor, I must attend annual meetings in the capital of Delhi. I was on my way there when my vehicle broke down. Your driver recognized me as King Norbu."

What are the odds?

I don't know about you, but I've met exactly zero kings. And Clayton didn't just meet a king, he met the king of the very village his team was trying to reach.

After revealing who he was, the king of Zangla asked Clayton's name. When he replied, "Clayton King," King Norbu took him literally! When he asked why an American king would visit his village, Clayton didn't pull any punches. He told the king that they wanted to set up a medical clinic and give his people copies of their holy book, the Bible. King Norbu was so pleased that he gave Clayton a handwritten letter that not only ensured safe passage and a warm reception in Zangla but also named Clayton the interim king while he was away. So when the team arrived in Zangla, they were treated like kings! Fancy that.

A Show of Power

The second day in the village, the queen asked Clayton if he knew how to deliver a baby. Of couse, he had no clue, but the doctor on their team did. She examined the mother and her twin babies, quickly assessing the situation. It was a tricky pregnancy to begin with, and in the doctor's professional opinion, one of the babies had already died in utero.

Clayton isn't sure what came over him in that moment, but he asked his interpreter to translate a message. As soon as he spoke the words, he felt the punch:

> We have come from America as the people of God. Our God is Jesus Christ, who was killed for our sins and then raised from the dead. He's powerful and loving, and He will show you His power. This mother will live tonight. And these babies will live tonight. God has sent us to you for this purpose. If they die, then you can do with us anything you wish.

In order to deliver the baby who was in a breech position, the doctor had to break his hip. Ouch. That enabled the baby to be born, but he was in fact stillborn. There was no pulse, no heartbeat, and no breath. They didn't know how long the baby had been dead, but Clayton did the only thing he knew how to do. He cried out to God. The next few minutes must have felt like four days, but the Grave Robber did it again. God raised the dead right in front of their eyes. They all saw he had no pulse and was blue as anything. But finally, the stillborn baby let out a scream that was music to their ears!

In cultures that are superstitious, God often reveals Himself with what missiologists call "a show of power." The showdown between Elijah and the prophets of Baal in 1 Kings 18 is a great example. It was like a prophetic cage fight. There was smack talk, there was a bet, and there were some heavy hitters. And just as God proved His superior power to the Baal worshipers, He proved His power to a village of Tibetan Buddhists by raising a baby from the dead.

Come Out

If you've read the Bible from cover to cover, you suffer from hindsight bias. You know how every story ends, so you lose the element of surprise. You lose the suspense and the raw emotion. That's *certainly* true of the seventh sign.

If you can, try to forget how this story ends. Seriously! This gets a paragraph break.

Now put yourself within earshot of Jesus when He says, "Lazarus, come out!"[7] You hear the words, but you can hardly believe your ears!

Who talks to dead people?

Because we assume the outcome—Lazarus walking out of the tomb—we fail to appreciate the risk Jesus took. If you're there, this just got real tense real fast. If you're one of His disciples, you gotta be second-guessing just a bit. If Lazarus stays dead, this is Jesus' most embarrassing moment. This could look even more like a cruel joke. Don't miss this little subplot in the story line.

The six miracles that precede this one certainly establish Jesus' credibility, but you're only as good as your last game or last performance. Athletes and entertainers know this. If Lazarus doesn't walk out of the tomb, Jesus' reputation is out the window. So when Jesus calls out, He's going all in and betting it all on Laz.

Second-Degree Faith

Let me double back to Martha's statement of faith:

> Lord . . . if you had been here, my brother would not have died. But I know that even now God will give you whatever you ask.[8]

This one statement reveals two types of faith.

The first half is *preventative faith*. Martha says, "Lord, if you had been here, my brother would not have died." Preventative faith believes God can keep things from happening. There's nothing wrong with not wanting to get hit by a bus or fall off a cliff, but there's a second dimension of faith that believes God can actually undo what's been done. You could call it *resurrection faith*. It's a faith that refuses to put periods at the end of disappointments. Even then you believe *even now*.

At some point, most of us end up with a dream that gets buried. That's true of nearly every dream God's ever given me. Crash and burn.

When I (Mark) was in college, I thought I might plant a church and pastor it for life. I've been living that dream for eighteen years as the lead pastor of National Community Church in Washington, DC, but there's a prequel. My first go at it was a flop.

When I was in seminary, the dream of planting a church in Chicago turned into a nightmare. The good news is that when that dream died, part of my ego died with it. Few things kill pride faster than failure! And that's the point.

There are times when you need to hang on to a dream for dear life, but there are also times when a dream needs to be laid to rest. It's tricky to know when to do what. I suppose Mary and Martha could have kept Lazarus lying in state on his deathbed instead of embalming him and laying him in the tomb. It's one thing raising the dead off of their deathbed. It's another thing calling a dead man out of a tomb four days postmortem. It's the best of all worlds, in a weird sort of way.

Sometimes you need to bury something.

If it's resurrected, you'll know it was the Grave Robber.

It takes courage to end a bad relationship. It takes courage to change majors or join a team or do whatever it is you need to do, but it's better to fail at something you love than succeed at something you hate. Maybe you need to bury the relationship, bury the job, bury the bottle, bury the clique, or bury the major. Then you just wait. He'll show up eventually, whether it's in four days, four years, or four seconds.

One Little Yes

Do you believe this?

John 11:26

The seventh miracle reveals the full-out, full-on Jesus. He's more than the Wine Maker or the Water Walker. He's the Grave Robber. And He saves His boldest claim for last:

I am the resurrection and the life.[1]

It's that unique claim that puts Him in a category by Himself: Son of God. No one else claims to be the Son of God. Christianity's not built on the foundation of philosophy or a code of ethics. The whole thing is based on one simple fact: an empty tomb. We know how it panned out with Lazarus, and, spoiler alert, He does the same thing later on with Himself.

If the resurrection didn't happen, Christianity ranks as history's cruelest hoax. We're just wasting our lives going after this guy. We're living a lie. But if Jesus walked out of the tomb two thousand years ago? Boom, there you have it. That's all, folks.

Remember Jefferson's Gospel? It comes to a screeching halt when the stone is rolled in front of the tomb on Good Friday. And I think that's where most people leave Jesus. Most people have no hesitation acknowledging that Jesus was compassionate and wise, a great teacher or a powerful prophet. But that ain't who He claimed to be. He claimed to be the *resurrection* and the *life*. And that's where people get stuck. But we're only left with two options: either Jesus was who He claimed to be or He wasn't.

In an interview with *Rolling Stone* magazine, Bono was asked his opinion on Jesus with this question: "Christ has his rank among the world's greatest thinkers. But Son of God, isn't that far-fetched?" The lead singer of U2 responded:

> No, it's not far-fetched to me. Look, the secular response to the Christ story always goes like this. He was a great prophet who had a lot to say along the lines of other great prophets, be they Elijah, Muhammad, Buddha, or Confucius. But actually Christ doesn't allow you that. He doesn't let you off that hook. Christ says, "No. I'm not saying I'm a teacher, don't call me a teacher. I'm not saying I'm a prophet. I'm saying: I'm the Messiah. I'm saying: I am God incarnate." And people say: No, no, please, just be a prophet. A prophet we can take. So what you're left with is either Christ was who he said he was—the Messiah—or a complete nutcase.[2]

Imagine a Jefferson vs. Bono debate. I'd pay to see that. I think Jefferson's the favorite by a long shot, but I think Bono wins this debate. While most people, like Jefferson, have no issue accepting Jesus as a compassionate healer or wise teacher or even a prophet, He claimed to be more than that. C. S. Lewis said it best: Jesus is either liar, lunatic, or Lord.[3]

There's no middle ground. Either Jesus is Lord of all or He's not Lord at all. So which is it?

One Little Yes

Jesus goes point-blank with Martha: "Do you believe this?"[4] Remember: Jesus hadn't called Lazarus out of the tomb quite yet, so Martha was still four days past hope. But she still drops her one little yes:

Yes, Lord.[5]

One little *yes* can change your life.
One little *yes* can change your eternity.

I think the only question on God's final exam is: *Do you believe this?* It's a little obvious when you're face-to-face with God, but still. It's not multiple-choice; it's true or false. That right there is the most important question you'll ever answer. The good news is that it's an open-book exam, and God reveals the right answer in Romans 10:9:

If you confess with your mouth that Jesus is Lord and believe in your heart that God raised him from the dead, you will be saved. (ESV)

The resurrection of Jesus Christ is all that matters. When He walked out of the tomb under His own power, *impossible* stopped being a thing. The resurrection is the history-changer, the game-changer. But the trick is learning to live as if Jesus was crucified yesterday, rose from the dead today, and is coming back tomorrow![6]

The resurrections don't even stop there. God resurrects dreams from the dead. He resurrects dead relationships. And no matter what part of your personality has died at the hands of sin or suffering, the Grave Robber came to give you your life back!

A few years ago I (Mark) had the privilege of baptizing a young woman whose life had been totally transformed. I'll never forget Rachel's face when she came back up out of the water. Rachel described it this way: "Now I'm the person I was as a child, always smiling and laughing."

When Jesus died on the cross, Satan smiled. But the Grave Robber got the last laugh. He always does. And if you give Him a chance, He'll give you a second chance.

He will give you your smile back.
He will give you your laugh back.
He will give you your life back.

Do you believe this?
If you do, He will make the impossible possible.

Notes

Chapter 1 Dear Water: Act More Like Wine

1. I'm indebted to Dorothy L. Sayers for this sentiment from her 1942 essay "Why Work?"

Chapter 2 Miraculous

1. Gene Weingarten, "Pearls Before Breakfast," *Washington Post*, April 8, 2007, http://www.washingtonpost.com/wp-dyn/content/article/2007/04/04/AR200704040 1721.html.

2. G. K. Chesterton, *Orthodoxy* (Nashville: Sam Torode Book Arts, 2008), 56.

3. Andrew Fraknoi, "How Fast Are You Moving When You Are Sitting Still?" *The Universe in the Classroom* 71 (Spring 2007), http://www.astrosociety.org/edu/publications/tnl/71/uitc071.pdf.

4. Carl Zimmer, "You're a Dim Bulb (And I Mean That in the Best Possible Way)," *The Loom* (blog), March 23, 2006, http://blogs.discovermagazine.com/loom/2006/03/23/youre-a-dim-bulb-and-i-mean-that-in-the-best-possible-way/#. UjNs67warzc.

5. Shlomo Katz, ed., Torah.org, *Hamaayan*, vol. X, no. 1, October 21, 1995, http://www.torah.org/learning/hamaayan/5756/bereishis.html.

Chapter 3 The Lost Miracles

1. For these and other facts about the Library of Congress, see "About the Library," Library of Congress, http://www.loc.gov/about/index.html.

2. Thomas Jefferson, The Thomas Jefferson Papers Series 1, General Correspondence, 1651–1827, Thomas Jefferson to John Adams, June 10, 1815, http://hdl.loc.gov/loc.mss/mtj.mtjbib022062.

3. Edwin Gaustad, *Sworn on the Altar of God* (Grand Rapids: Eerdmans, 1996), 129.

4. Ibid., 130.

5. See Joshua 3.

6. See 2 Kings 5:14.

7. Laurence Gonzales, *Deep Survival* (New York: W. W. Norton, 2003), 52–53.

8. Mark 9:24 ESV.

9. John 20:31.

10. The exact quote is, "Every now and then a man's mind is stretched by a new idea or sensation, and never shrinks back to its former dimensions." From Oliver Wendell Holmes, *The Autocrat of the Breakfast-Table* (Boston: James R. Osgood and Co., 1873); online at Project Gutenberg, http://www.gutenberg.org/ebooks/751.

Chapter 4 The Wine Maker

1. Luke 2:47 ESV.

2. Luke 23:34 ESV.

3. Graham Greene, *The Power and the Glory* (London: Vintage Books, 2005), chap. 1.

4. See Luke 2:19.

5. See Psalm 8:5.

6. John 2:3 ESV.

Chapter 5 Six Stone Jars

1. Water makes up between 55–78 percent of body weight, with 65 percent being a median.

2. "Water Facts," Water.org, 2014, http://water.org/water-crisis/water-facts/water/, accessed January 6, 2014.

3. John 2:3 ESV.

4. Justin Voda, "Da Vinci-Inspired Pump Brings Water to Thousands," *OCCC Pioneer*, April 16, 2012, http://pioneer2010.occc.edu/index.php/clubs/68-clubs/2016-da-vinci-inspired-pump-brings-water-to-thousands.

5. Learn about the Water4 Foundation at http://water4.org/.

6. John 2:10 ESV.

7. "LEGO," Brickipedia.com, http://lego.wikia.com/wiki/LEGO, accessed January 7, 2014.

8. S.v. "ethanol fermentation," Wikipedia.com, modified December 31, 2013, http://en.wikipedia.org/wiki/Ethanol_fermentation.

9. Genesis 1:3.

10. Abraham Kuyper, "Sphere Sovereignty," in *Abraham Kuyper: A Centennial Reader*, James D. Bratt, ed. (Grand Rapids: Eerdmans, 1998), 488.

11. Colossians 1:16–17.

12. Matthew 26:28.

13. See Hebrews 9:22.

14. 2 Corinthians 5:21.

Chapter 6 God Speed

1. Henry Greene, "Wherever You Go," *Central Press* newsletter, Central Presbyterian Church, October 2013, http://www.cpcmerced.org/uploads/CentralPress October2013.pdf.

Chapter 7 The Seventh Hour

1. Tony Snesko, personal email to the author, used by permission.
2. Ibid.
3. Dallas Willard, *The Great Omission: Reclaiming Jesus's Essential Teachings on Discipleship* (Oxford, UK: Lion Hudson, 2006), 61.
4. See Luke 8:43–48.
5. See Luke 7:36–50.
6. See Mark 2:1–12.
7. See Mark 8:22–26.
8. Mark 8:25 ESV.
9. John 4:46.

Chapter 8 Very Superstitious

1. "The Unsolvable Math Problem," Snopes.com, updated June 28, 2011, http://www.snopes.com/college/homework/unsolvable.asp.
2. George Dantzig, http://en.wikipedia.org/wiki/George_Dantzig.
3. Matthew 19:26.
4. John 5:8.
5. Sarah Young, *Jesus Calling* (Nashville: Thomas Nelson, 2004), 243.
6. Email to the author, used by permission.
7. One of many versions of this story appears at "Ty Cobb," Baseball-statistics.com, http://www.baseball-statistics.com/HOF/Cobb.html.
8. See Joshua 10.
9. See 2 Kings 6.
10. See Luke 1.
11. See Matthew 14.
12. See John 11:25.

Chapter 9 Self-Fulfilling Prophecies

1. John 5:6.
2. See Luke 23:39.
3. See 2 Kings 5.
4. See Luke 8:42–48.
5. See John 21.
6. "Understanding Motion by Standing Still," Boston University, January 16, 1998, http://www.newswise.com/articles/understanding-motion-by-standing-still.
7. See Daniel 1. I also recommend *The Daniel Plan: 40 Days to a Healthier Life* by Rick Warren, Dr. Daniel Amen, and Dr. Mark Hyman (Grand Rapids: Zondervan, 2013).

8. See Romans 8:37.
9. See Zechariah 2:8.
10. See Isaiah 62:12.
11. See Romans 8:17.
12. See John 1:12.
13. See Matthew 16:18.
14. "They'll Put a Man on the Moon before I Hit a Home Run," Did You Know?, May 4, 2011, http://didyouknow.org/theyll-put-a-man-on-the-moon-before-i-hit-a-home-run/.
15. Alex Santoso, "Jim Carrey Once Wrote Himself a $10 Million Check," Neatorama, October 7, 2012, http://www.neatorama.com/2012/10/07/Jim-Carrey-Once-Wrote-Himself-a-10-Million-Check/.
16. Acts 3:6.
17. Thanks to Eugene Peterson for this idea, inspired by his book *A Long Obedience in the Same Direction: Discipleship in an Instant Society* (Downers Grove, IL: InterVarsity, 1980).

Chapter 10 Two Fish

1. John 6:5.
2. John 6:7.
3. See Psalm 50:10.
4. Oswald Chambers, *My Utmost for His Highest* (Grand Rapids: Discovery House, 2006), 13.
5. Matthew 6:11 NKJV.
6. John 6:10.

Chapter 11 Count the Fish

1. John 6:6.
2. See Mark 8:1–10.
3. John 6:9.
4. See John 21:1–14.
5. Luke 5:5.

Chapter 12 The Water Walker

1. Mark 4:39 NKJV.
2. Lindsey Konkel, "Could Humans Walk on Water?" Livescience.com, June 29, 2010, http://www.livescience.com/32670-could-humans-walk-on-water.html.
3. Doron Nof, Ian McKeague, and Nathan Paldor, "Is There a Paleolimnological Explanation for 'Walking on Water' in the Sea of Galilee?" *Journal of Paleolimnology* 35 (2006), 417–39. The authors make an admission along with this assertion: "Whether this happened or not is an issue for religion scholars, archeologists, anthropologists, and believers to decide on. As natural scientists, we merely point out that unique freezing processes probably happened in that region several times during the last 12,000 years."

4. Al Seckel, "Al Seckel: Visual Illusions That Show How We (Mis)Think," TED.com, February 2004 (posted April 2007), http://www.ted.com/talks/al_seckel_says_our_brains_are_mis_wired.html.

5. Richard Restak, *Mozart's Brain and the Fighter Pilot: Unleashing Your Brain's Potential* (New York: Harmony, 2001), 92.

6. Mark Nepo, *The Book of Awakening* (San Francisco: Conari Press, 2000), 131.

7. "*Star Trek* Quotes," IMDB.com, 2014, http://www.imdb.com/title/tt0060028/quotes.

8. John 3:8 ESV.

Chapter 13 Dare the Devil

1. See Matthew 21:12–13.

2. Dorothy Sayers, *The Greatest Drama Ever Staged: Letters to a Diminished Church* (Nashville: Thomas Nelson, 2004).

3. See Mark 5:1–20.

4. 1 John 4:18 ESV.

5. John 6:18.

6. André Gide, *The Counterfeiters: A Novel*, trans. Dorothy Bussy (New York: Vintage Books, 1973), 353.

7. See John 6:19.

Chapter 14 Never Say Never

1. Oliver Sacks, *The Island of the Colorblind* (New York: Vintage Books, 1998), 208.

2. Luke 11:34 ESV.

3. *Pneumatology* is theology of the Holy Spirit. *Soteriology* is theology of salvation. *Eschatology* is theology of the end times.

4. Albert Einstein, "Religion and Science," *New York Times Magazine*, November 9, 1930, 1–4; online at http://www.sacred-texts.com/aor/einstein/einsci.htm.

5. Quoted in David N. Menton, "The Eye," BestBibleScience.org, http://www.bestbiblescience.org/eye.htm.

6. Proverbs 20:12.

7. Bradley Voktek, "Are There Really as Many Neurons in the Human Brain as Stars in the Milky Way?," *Brain Metrics* (blog), May 20, 2013, http://www.nature.com/scitable/blog/brain-metrics/are_there_really_as_many.

Chapter 15 The Miracle League

1. See Matthew 9:20–22.

2. John Tiller, testimony at National Community Church, used by permission.

3. Ibid.

4. John 9:2.

5. John 9:3.

6. Hebrews 11:32–35.

7. Hebrews 11:35–38.

8. Max Lucado shares JJ's story in his book *You'll Get through This: Hope and Help for Your Turbulent Times* (Nashville: Thomas Nelson, 2013), 23–24.

9. Ibid., 28.

10. "Mississippi Television Station WCBI Airs Flame On Story," *Flame On Blog*, March 9, 2011, http://www.flameon.net/blog/mississippi-television-station-wcbi-airs-flame-on-story.aspx.

11. Quoted in ibid.

12. Dr. Martin Seligman, *Learned Optimism* (New York: A. A. Knopf, 1991).

13. Genesis 50:20.

14. Aldous Huxley, *Texts and Pretexts* (New York: W. W. Norton, 1962), 5.

15. Romans 8:28.

16. See John 9:7.

17. As quoted by Rodney Buchanan in his sermon "Blindness and Light," Sermon Central, July 2007, http://www.sermoncentral.com/sermons/blindness--light-rodney-buchanan-sermon-on-faith-general-109700.asp.

18. John 9:7 ESV.

Chapter 16 The Grave Robber

1. Genesis 2:17.

2. John 11:44.

3. "What Happened to Lazarus after His Resurrection?" The Straight Dope, October 20, 2009, http://www.straightdope.com/columns/read/2902/what-happened-to-lazarus-after-his-resurrection.

4. See John 10:10.

5. 1 Corinthians 15:55.

6. See 2 Corinthians 5:8.

Chapter 17 Even Now

1. John 11:15.

2. John 11:21, 32.

3. John 11:4.

4. Oswald Chambers, "The Big Compelling of God," in *My Utmost for His Highest*, http://utmost.org/classic/the-big-compelling-of-god-classic/.

5. John 11:21–22.

6. Clayton told me this story in person, but you can read his amazing account in his book *Amazing Encounters with God: Stories to Open Your Eyes to His Power* (Eugene, OR: Harvest House, 2009).

7. John 11:43.

8. John 11:21–22.

Chapter 18 One Little Yes

1. John 11:25.

2. Michka Assayas, *Bono: In Conversation with Michka Assayas* (New York: Riverhead, 2005), 205.

3. C. S. Lewis, *Mere Christianity* (1952; repr., New York: HarperCollins, 2001), 54.

4. John 11:26.

5. John 11:27.

6. Thanks to Martin Luther for this thought. He said, "Preach as if Jesus was crucified yesterday, rose from the dead today, and is coming back tomorrow."

Mark Batterson is the *New York Times* bestselling author of *The Circle Maker*. The lead pastor of National Community Church in Washington, DC, Mark has a doctor of ministry degree from Regent University and lives on Capitol Hill with his wife, Lora, and their three children.

Parker Batterson is studying film production at Southeastern University in Lakeland, Florida. He is also the coauthor of the student editions of *The Circle Maker* and *All In*.